T0360727

Food Advertising and Childhood Obesity

This book explores the ways in which the environmental factor of advertising can influence children's food choice and health status, and how it contributes to the significant public health issue of childhood obesity.

Food Advertising and Childhood Obesity seeks to gain a better understanding of children's food choice based on children's exposure to different advertising by analyzing food type, brand mascot physique, health messages, and media. The book begins by reviewing the ways in which children become consumers and the role of advertising in this process. It then explores a range of advertising variables in children's food choice and consumption. This includes theoretical and practical discussion of foods and brand mascots, health messages embodied in food advertising, and comparisons of the effects of different advertising based on entertainment level, such as using new media to present 'advergames' supported by television advertising. Each chapter is supported with relevant theories and a research summary is presented on each topic for clarification. The book also introduces some ways of constructive working with children and concludes with a chapter dedicated to market research and children.

Written for students and practitioners of marketing, market research, and advertising, especially within the global food industry, this book offers readers a new approach to understanding child food choice and consumption that will inform effective corporate social responsibility strategies to address this issue.

Fariba Esmaeilpour works as chief executive officer at Salaam Institute, a research NGO with the aim of finding ways to design effective social marketing programs targeted to children. She is also a marketing lecturer.

Mitra Shabani Nashtaee is Assistant Professor of Marketing in the Department of Business Management at Islamic Azad University (Roudbar branch, Roudbar, Iran).

Routledge Studies in Marketing

This series welcomes proposals for original research projects that are either single or multi-authored or an edited collection from both established and emerging scholars working on any aspect of marketing theory and practice and provides an outlet for studies dealing with elements of marketing theory, thought, pedagogy and practice.

It aims to reflect the evolving role of marketing and bring together the most innovative work across all aspects of the marketing 'mix' – from product development, consumer behaviour, marketing analysis, branding, and customer relationships, to sustainability, ethics and the new opportunities and challenges presented by digital and online marketing.

Strategic Brand Management in Higher Education
Edited by Bang Nyugen, T.C Melewar and Jane Hemsley-Brown

Digital Disruption in Marketing and Communications
A Strategic and Organizational Approach
Edoardo Magnotta

Branding and Positioning in Base of Pyramid Markets in Africa
Innovative Approaches
Charles Blankson and Stanley Coffie

Strategic Marketing of Higher Education in Africa
Edited by Emmanuel Mogaji, Felix Maringe and Robert Ebo Hinson

Food Advertising and Childhood Obesity
Examining Food Type, Brand Mascot Physique, Health Message, and Media
Fariba Esmaeilpour and Mitra Shabani Nashtaee

For more information about this series, please visit www.routledge.com/ Routledge-Studies-in-Marketing/book-series/RMKT

Food Advertising and Childhood Obesity

Examining Food Type, Brand Mascot
Physique, Health Message, and Media

**Fariba Esmaeilpour and
Mitra Shabani Nashtaee**

LONDON AND NEW YORK

First published 2020
by Routledge
2 Park Square, Milton Park, Abingdon, Oxon OX14 4RN

and by Routledge
52 Vanderbilt Avenue, New York, NY 10017

Routledge is an imprint of the Taylor & Francis Group, an informa business

British Library Cataloguing-in-Publication Data
A catalogue record for this book is available from the British Library

Library of Congress Cataloging-in-Publication Data
Names: Esmaeilpour, Fariba, author. | Nashtaee, Mitra Shabani, author.
Title: Food advertising and childhood obesity : examining food
    type, brand mascot physique, health message and media / Fariba
    Esmaeilpour and Mitra Shabani Nashtaee.
Description: Abingdon, Oxon ; New York, NY : Routledge,
    2020. | Series: Routledge studies in marketing ; 10 | Includes
    bibliographical references and index.
Identifiers: LCCN 2019052706 (print) | LCCN 2019052707 (ebook) |
    ISBN 9780367361877 (hardback) | ISBN 9780429344435 (ebook)
Subjects: LCSH: Advertising and children—Health aspects. |
    Obesity in children. | Advertising—Food—Health aspects. |
    Nutrition in mass media.
Classification: LCC HF5415.332.C45 E86 2020 (print) | LCC
    HF5415.332.C45 (ebook) | DDC 614.5/99292398—dc23
LC record available at https://lccn.loc.gov/2019052706
LC ebook record available at https://lccn.loc.gov/2019052707

ISBN: 978-0-367-36187-7 (hbk)
ISBN: 978-0-429-34443-5 (ebk)

Typeset in Times New Roman
by Apex CoVantage, LLC

Contents

Preface

Childhood overweightness and obesity is a significant public health issue. Obesity is now considered the fifth leading global risk factor contributing to mortality and has reached an epidemic status. Meanwhile, an unhealthy diet is one of the four key preventable risk factors for non-communicable disease, the leading cause of death globally. Unhealthy diets are a major contributor to the twin non-communicable disease epidemics of type 2 diabetes and obesity. Overweight children are more likely to become overweight adults and experience many health problems, including cardiovascular disease, metabolic syndrome, asthma, acid reflux, orthopedic problems, depression, type 2 diabetes, heart disease, stroke, and some cancers. Of particular concern is the emergence of these nutrition-related conditions among children and young people. In addition to the relationship between childhood diet and chronic disease in adulthood, reasons such as an increasing number of mothers working outside the home, the lack of day care centers for children, growth retardation, the prevalence of some nutritional deficiencies such as anemia, and deficiency of energy and protein have led to more attention to the diet of children.

With changes in dietary habits and activity levels, the prevalence of obesity is increasing not only in developed countries, but also in developing countries. The position of developing countries in an epidemiological transition along with fast changes in eating patterns and an inclination to high-energy and low-nutritional-value foods have led to the emergence of a phenomenon in these countries that has been called 'Lifestyle Syndrome' or 'New World Syndrome'. Parallel to these changes and with consideration of the fact that many health-related behaviors are formed during childhood, much attention has been paid to primordial prevention of behavioral and biological risk factors of chronic diseases in adulthood.

At the macro level, nutritional problems threaten the development process of the country with adverse social, economic, and health consequences including increased mortality and morbidity, increased treatment costs, decreased IQ and learning power, reduced work power, and generally reduced mental and physical abilities. Among the various factors of nutritional problems and the prevalence of obesity, marketing (and especially advertising) has been identified as a very influential environmental factor on the diet of children. Therefore, during the last decade, consumer groups, parents, teachers' professional associations, and public health advocacy organizations have called for greater control over the marketing of foods and beverages to children. Since the basis of nutritional habits is formed in childhood, creating proper awareness and attitudes in children through appropriate education methods seems necessary, and promoting the health of this vulnerable group will be able to prevent the spread of non-communicable disease in developing countries.

However, advertising has provided some reasons to eliminate these criticisms. For example, in response to the question of 'are marketing and advertising necessary?' by critics, marketers answer that based on the economics of information perspective, advertising is an important source of consumer information. Advertising only helps one to notice the availability of products to meet existing needs. Accordingly, advertising is a service for which consumers are willing to pay because the information it provides reduces their search time. On the other hand, the irrational focus of consumers on goods that are symbolic are largely the result of the socialization process of individuals in the family and in the general environment rather than marketing.

The purpose of this book is not to accuse marketing and advertising of creating the syndrome of the new world, of which prevalence of obesity in children is a characteristic, and not to provide reasons for defending marketing and eliminating its charge. Instead, this book attempts to provide reports in the form of theories and research findings on the relationship between the main variables of food advertising (including products, characters, messages, and entertainment levels) and children's food choice. The judgment will be the responsibility of the reader.

1 Children as consumers

In 2013, 2.1 billion people worldwide were overweight or obese, including one in five children and adolescents aged 5 to 17 years in several high- and middle-income countries. According to the World Health Organization's (WHO) estimation, more than 40 million children under the age of 5 years were overweight or obese in 2012 which, with current trends, may reach 70 million by 2025.

Food choice is one of the areas where children have gained major influence. This has caused concern about consuming diets high in fat and sugar but low in essential nutrients such as calcium, iron, and possibly antioxidant vitamins, which could have both short- and long-term adverse effects on children's health. In other words, since children increasingly have more choice over the food that they consume, this may lead to diets of poor nutritional value. The pattern of food choice and consumption during childhood as a health-related behavior not only influences children's quality of life but also likely persists in adulthood.

Children: consumers-in-training

Children are the largest market segment, and in many parts of the world they are more involved in choosing what to buy, use, and eat than they have ever been before. In today's demanding economic climate where marketers face the challenge of growing brands and businesses, marketers look to the children's market as a place to find new or increased current and future revenue. Since nobody has more lifetime value as a consumer than a child, the children's market was always considered to be the market with the most growth potential. However, the world children live in has changed during recent decades and they now play a modified role in their families and in society to the point where marketers owe it to themselves to take a second look at children's new acquired economic power. The days when children should be seen and not heard are long gone. They have more personal power, more money, more influence, and attention than any other generation before them. They've grown up faster and are more connected, more direct, and more informed.

Children make up three distinct segments including the primary, influence, and future markets. As a primary market, they represent a huge market for toys, apparel, and even electronics in that more than half of children aged 8 to 12 have their own cellphone and there are numerous tablets designed for them as well.

The influence market emerges when parents buy what their children tell them to buy. When a parental decision maker surrenders to a child's request, parental yielding occurs. The likelihood of parental yielding occurring partly depends on the dynamics within a particular family. Parents have styles ranging from permissive to strict, and also vary in terms of the amount of responsibility children are given to make decisions.

Social power theory, as an appropriate theoretical framework to study children's direct influence attempts, identifies the bases of power that are present in social interactions. This theory suggests that a person will make an assessment of his or her resources and choose an influence attempt that is consistent with his or her sources of social power. According to the conceptual framework of social power theory, children's influence may be divided into two categories: direct (i.e. active) and indirect (i.e. passive). In a direct influence attempt, the agent's actions are intended to affect a change in behavior, attitude, goal, need, or value on the part of the target. In parent-child interactions, a direct influence attempt is related to the sum of a child's actions intended to direct a decision outcome according to his or her own preferences. In passive influence, a parent's perception of a child's unstated preferences influences a purchase decision. Unlike the passive influence, a direct influence attempt encompasses only those instances where a child takes goal-directed action toward influencing a decision. Direct influence is multidimensional and includes different influence strategies. Fourteen types of children's power strategies – including asking, begging and pleading, telling or assertion, reasoning, demanding or arguing, state importance, bargaining, persistence, negative affect, positive affect, verbal manipulation, eliciting reciprocity, using an advocate, evasion, and laissez-faire – were found by Cowan et al. Cowan and Avants also identified strategies of ask, bargain, positive feelings, do as I please, tell, negative feelings, persistence, beg and plead, good deeds, reasoning, cry, and get angry.

Children are also considered a future market. They grow up quickly and purchase items such as photographic equipment and cell phones that adults normally purchase. Smart marketers are looking to establish brand loyalty at an early age. 'Consumer socialization' and 'consumer development' is how children become consumers.

Consumer socialization

The term socialization refers to processes by which individuals learn to participate effectively in the social environment. Zigler and Child use the term this way:

> Socialization is a broad term for the whole process by which an individual develops, through transaction with other people, his specific patterns of socially relevant behaviors and experience.

Socialization is related to the learning of social roles and the behavior associated with those roles. Accordingly, consumer socialization is the processes by which young people acquire skills, knowledge, and attitudes relevant to their functioning as consumers in the marketplace. The focus of this definition is on childhood socialization, not on all learning that takes place during this period of time. Also, the discussion is limited to marketplace transactions. It means that the focus is on consumption-relevant skills, knowledge, and attitudes. In addition, there is a distinction between skills, knowledge, and attitudes that are directly relevant to consumption behavior; and skills, knowledge, and attitudes that are indirectly relevant to consumption behavior. Directly relevant skills, knowledge, and attitudes are used for enactment of the consumer role. Some examples are skills at budgeting, pricing, knowledge of brand attitudes and shopping outlets, and attitudes toward products, brands, and salespeople. Consumer role enactment may occur during the physical act of purchasing. It also can refer to the set of physical and mental activities specifically involved in purchase decisions, talking to others about products and brands, and weighing purchase criteria. However, more importantly for many consumption behaviors are the indirectly relevant skills, knowledge, and attitudes that motivate purchases. For example, a college student who purchases a dark suit for a business interview is acting according to perceived norms and role requirements associated with job interviews. For understanding the purchase, the knowledge and attitudes concerning the interview situation norms and associated role requirements are important.

Consumer socialization research is dominated by four main theoretical approaches including cognitive development theory, social development theory, interpersonal communication theory, and learning theory. These approaches will be explained next.

Cognitive development theories

According to cognitive development theories that stem from the work of Jean Piaget, socialization is a function of qualitative changes in one's cognitive organization between infancy and adulthood. These change stages are based on cognitive structures used by the child in perceiving and coping with the environment at different ages. Four main stages of Piaget's cognitive development theory are sensorimotor (birth to 2 years), preoperational (2 to 7 years), concrete operational (7 to 11 years), and formal operational (after 11 years). Differences of these stages are in terms of abilities and resources available to children. Between stages, consumer researchers focus on three last stages including preoperational, concrete operational, and formal operational. Children's symbolic thought develops in the preoperational stage but is still very focused on perceptual properties of stimuli. In the preoperational stage, children tend to be perceptually bound to the readily observable aspects of their environment. Centration (i.e. the tendency to focus on a single dimension) is another characteristic of preoperational children. In contrast, in the concrete operational stage, children can consider several dimensions of a stimulus at a time and relate those dimensions in a thoughtful and relatively abstract way. Finally, in the formal operational stage, children move to more adult-like thought patterns and are capable of even more complex thought about concrete and hypothetical objects and situations.

Among cognitive development theories, information processing theories also provide explanatory power for the types of children's cognitive abilities as they mature. Although there are several formulations of information processing theory, all of them focus on children's developing skills in the areas of acquisition, encoding, organizing, and retrieval of information. Accordingly, based on their information-processing skills, children are considered as belonging to one of three segments: strategic processors, cued processors, or limited processors. Strategic processors (age 12 and older) use a variety of strategies such as verbal labeling, rehearsal, and use of retrieval cues to guide memory search for storing and retrieving information. Cued processors (from 7 to 11 years) use a similar set of strategies to enhance information storage and retrieval, but typically need to be aided by explicit prompts or cues. In other words, they have the ability to use processing strategies but do not spontaneously produce these strategies when needed. Finally, limited processors' (under the age of seven) processing skills are not yet fully developed or successfully utilized in learning situations. These processors often have difficulty using storage and retrieval strategies even when prompted to do so.

The cognitive development stages provide a basis for explaining the emergence of a variety of socialization outcomes. For example, children's ability to distinguish advertising (as a persuasive means) from television programming grows during these stages. Information processing views also explain this finding in terms of children's abilities to retrieve and use information.

Social development theory

Social development includes a wide variety of topics such as moral development, altruism and pro-social development, impression formation, and social perspective taking. Among these topics, social perspective taking and impression formation are the most directly relevant to consumer socialization. For example, social perspective taking – the ability of seeing perspectives beyond one's own – is strongly related to purchase influence and negotiation skills. Impression formation – the ability of making social comparisons – can also help with understanding the social aspects of products and consumption.

Social perspective taking describes how children's abilities to understand different perspectives progress through a series of stages. In the egocentric stage (ages 3 to 6), children are unaware of any point of view other than their own. As they grow, in the social informational role-taking stage (ages 6 to 8), children become aware that others may have different opinions or motives because of having different information. However, they do not still consider the different perspectives on the situation as the reason for having different opinions. Thus, children in the social informational role-taking stage do not have the ability to actually think from another person's perspective. This ability surfaces in the stage of self-reflective role taking (ages 8 to 10). In this stage, children not only understand that others may have different opinions or motives but also can actually consider another person's viewpoint. The ability of simultaneously considering another person's viewpoint at the same time as one's own emerges in the fourth stage of mutual role taking (ages 10 to 12). In the stage of social and conventional system role taking (ages 12 to 15 and older), children acquire the ability to understand another person's perspective as a member of the social group or a person who work for the social system.

Barenboim, through impression formation, provided a description of the developmental sequence that takes place from 6 to 12 years of age. Barenboim believed that children describe other people in concrete or absolute terms before the age of 6. They often mention physical appearances or overt behaviors. In Barenboim's first stage, the behavioral comparisons phase (ages 6 to 8), children do incorporate comparisons as a basis of their impressions. These comparisons continue based on concrete attributes or behaviors. In the second stage, the psychological constructs phase (ages 8 to 10), impressions are based on psychological or abstract attributes, but do not include comparisons to others. In the psychological comparisons phase (ages 11 to 12 and older), comparisons are done based on psychological or abstract attributes, and children exhibit more adult-like impressions.

Interpersonal communications theory

According to all definitions of interpersonal communications, at least two people must be involved and an object of communication must be present. Social communication theorists can be divided roughly between those who are concerned with the interactants' cognitive orientations to events and issues in the world outside their immediate context (A-X and B-X relationships) and those who stress elements of interpersonal relationships (A-B relationships). It seems that consumer socialization proceeds more through subtle interpersonal processes than through direct and purposive consumer training in families or schools. Purposive consumer training by parents occurs infrequently and parents have only general consumer goals for their children such as teaching children about price-quality relationships. Although informal interpersonal communication processes occur in several types of social settings (e.g. with peers, siblings, or parents), the family context of interpersonal communication have the greatest influence in consumer socialization.

Family communication is the overt interactions between family members. This communication, which is concerned with participation in family consumer tasks and decisions, influences children's attitudes toward advertising and increases their economic motivations for consumption. Peer communication is also the overt peer-adolescent interactions and is conceptualized as encouragement or approval of certain behaviors and intentions through either spoken (reinforcement) or unspoken (modeling) messages that peers send to each other. This communication has a significant influence on attitudes toward advertising, materialistic values, and social motivations for consumption. Peers can have a significant effect on children's product evaluation.

Learning theory

Almost all definitions of socialization share at least one common element that is variously expressed in verb form as 'acquires', 'develops', or 'transmits'. This element means that socialization results in a relatively permanent change in the behavior of an individual. The generic term for this relatively permanent change is 'learning'. In consumer socialization, there is not an agreement about employing learning theories because formal learning theories are different in terms of process, content, and goal.

As purposive consumer training rarely occurs in families, children may learn certain consumer skills through observation and imitation. According to Bandura's argument, such learning processes explain how material objects acquire social meaning through mass media advertising. Observed rewards increase and observed punishments decrease imitative behavior. This is a widely applied technique in advertising appeals, as following the recommended action results in a host of rewarding outcomes. Meanwhile, a particular concern is the potential of television to teach violence to children. Children may imitate new methods of aggression displayed in television shows and movies.

Understanding of consumer socialization processes could be used as an input to consumer education programs. For example, a learning theory perspective can be used to answer the question of 'what socialization processes occur within low-income subcultures?' Children from low-income homes usually have less experience with money and may be less aware of the range of consumer goods. Therefore, their learning of some aspects of consumer skills should be less adequate than children from upper-income homes with more opportunities for consumption. On the other hand, children from low-income homes are more likely to become highly skilled consumers because they have had to learn disciplined uses of scarce resources.

Children's development as consumers

Learning is a developmental process that proceeds through a series of stages as children mature into adult consumers. Children acquire knowledge and decision-making skills regarding products, brands, advertising, shopping, pricing, parental influence strategies, and consumption motives and values during these stages. Children can also learn consumer behavior patterns in absence of other social actors, through interacting with environmental influences such as products, packaging, communication tools, and point-of-purchase displays. Although children have the ability to learn autonomously through interacting with their physical environment, parents mediate their exposure to marketing, communication, and retail stimuli.

Children are eager to understand their physical and social environment. Their level of understanding determines different aspects of children's consumer behavior such as their preferences for products, information, and entertainment. Infants through age 2 can feel wants and preferences. Newborns prefer sweet substances rather than sour, salty, or bitter ones. In other words, they are born with some very definitive preferences for tastes and smells. They have an innate tendency to the human voice, especially attentive to a 'motherese' form: a slower pace, higher pitch, and greatly exaggerated intonations. Despite children's distinct preferences for smells, colors, sounds, objects, and images in this period, their behavior is still primarily reactive and not very intentional.

In preschool ages (age 2 to 5; the period of nagging and negotiating), children's minds have some characteristics that determine their consumer behavior. For example, they have limited ability to distinguish fantasy from reality. A 2- or 3-year-old child often thinks that television characters reside inside the TV set. Children in these ages think that the information in commercials is true and do not often understand the persuasive intent of advertising. Because of limited cognitive capacity, they need more time than adults to interpret and make sense of information. Therefore, young preschoolers often respond best to programs with a slow pace and lots of repetition. Centration is another characteristic of preschool-aged children that may influence their consumer behavior: they have a tendency to center attention on one aspect of everything. Also, they cannot keep their minds off tempting products for long.

Although early elementary school children (age 5 to 8; adventure and the first purchase stage) still have many of the characteristics of preschoolers, a number of changes occur in these ages. In these ages, children's attention span becomes considerably larger and development of imaginative play reaches its peak. They also develop a preference for more fast-paced entertainment during these years and show persistence with content that is more difficult to understand because of their new acquired ability to make sense of far more information. Some other characteristics of this age group are more responsiveness to verbally oriented information and entertainment; more complicated characters; and more sophisticated forms of humor. Around age 5, children make their first independent purchases, usually in a supermarket or department store together with the parent.

In later elementary school children (ages 8 to 12; the stage of conformity and fastidiousness), peers' opinions play an increasingly important role. In this period children's eye for detail and quality develops, and they are able to critically evaluate and compare products and information. Their fantasies more often entail realistic and plausible themes, and they develop a sincere interest in real-world phenomena. So, they become highly critical of unrealistic entertainment and commercials. They also obtain the ability to decenter, and thereby come to consider and focus on details. Because of this emergent eye for detail and quality, some children in this age group develop a preference for collecting objects, such as dolls or cards of their heroes. In the later elementary school years, children's ability to recognize and interpret others' emotions improves rapidly, and as a result their requests for advertised products decrease by age 9 or 10 as well. In other words, they become more critical about media offerings, but their sensitivity to peer influences reaches its peak in this period. In this stage, children's influence on household purchases increases due to their increased loyalty to brand names and their increased negotiation strategies. Children's consumer behavior continues to develop during adolescence and adulthood, but they have almost become familiar with all aspects of their consumer behavior by age 12. As was explained previously, they are able to feel wants and preferences from infancy and toddlerhood; search to fulfill them from the preschool period; make a choice and a purchase from the early elementary school period; and evaluate a product and its alternatives from the later elementary school period.

Dichotomous child theory

According to dichotomous child theory, on the one hand, children can be considered as passive and vulnerable subjects who need protection. On the other hand, they are considered as sort of heroic figures who have the power of making unique and original meanings out of every piece of culture. Therefore at the same time, they can be both active and passive. Marketers overemphasize the active role of children as consumers in order to justify marketing decisions in terms of being ethical. It should be considered that although children have the ability to engage in autonomous and creative behaviors, they are still dependent subjects whose conduct is restricted by precise physical, cognitive, and social constraints.

On the one hand, critics of capitalism and consumer culture discuss the exploited view; and on the other hand, those who believe that children are active and agentive beings generally reject the role and place of consumption and media in children's lives. As a significant exception, Elizabeth Chin's ethnography of poor African-American girls finds both empowerment and exploitation in children's lives as consumers. While empowerment often came from the act of consuming, exploitation was the result of race and poverty. Due to this dichotomy of the child consumer, it should be asked 'what children know or don't know' and 'what children do or can't do' when they act alone.

In today's economic climate, children are important, precious, and knowing targets with usually unheard voices that need to be empowered. They almost effortlessly find expressions of self in the advertisements, packaging, and other materials of promotional culture. Children have gained increasing levels and kinds of legitimacy as social persons through participation in the consumer marketplace. Most children cannot afford and do not have the possibility to purchase the goods they possess or want. Meanwhile, parents find themselves as obstacles to their own child's realization of self in this sense and marketers use this contemporary ideology as a way to neutralize parental resistance.

Research sample

Title

The perception of media messages by preschool children.

Objective

The mass media, especially in today's world with the increased growth of digital technology, plays a significant role in human life and society. Through these media, as an important socialization factor, children learn social roles and the behavior associated with those roles. These media are also used to acquire skills, knowledge, and attitudes relevant to children functioning as consumers in the marketplace. Accordingly, the aim of this study was to ascertain how children consume media, which types of media content they are sensitive to, and how children affect the shopping behavior of their parents. In detail, this study was looking for revealing distinctions among the selection of the media, preferences of media products and forms, concepts within advertising, attractiveness of media content, types of influence of advertising products, and the means by which boys and girls have an impact on their parents.

Method

In this study, an exploratory research method was used with the purpose of determining the target areas. The emphasis of the research was on capturing the range of relevant topics concerning the researched issue.

Data were collected through semi-structured interviews with every participant. Each interview took about 30 minutes. The interviews were carried out with children and their parents individually in their households or in kindergartens. In order to obtain more enriched data, children were asked to draw an advertisement. In drawings, only the products and advertising topics that children focused on were noticed.

Fifty-five children (25 boys and 30 girls) aged 2 to 7 (in the preoperational stage of cognitive development) participated in the study using a snowball sampling method from the Czech Republic. The data were gathered in November and December because these months are before Christmas; the time that the media puts pressure on children for shopping for Christmas gifts could be manipulated by advertising in the media.

To analyze the data, a six-stage framework of thematic content analysis was used. The stages involved were: a) familiarizing with data through repeating reading; b) generating initial codes based on themes' location and relation to research questions; c) searching for main overarching themes and sub-themes within them; d) reviewing and refining themes to visualize a thematic map; e) defining and naming themes to identify the story of each theme and to consider its fitness into the broader overall; and finally f) providing sufficient evidence of the themes within the data.

To observe the principles of studies involving children, ethical principles of the British Psychological Society and American Psychological Association (APA) regarding research with children were respected. To respect the principle of consent, the interviews were completely voluntary and participants were actively involved in the conversations. Also, parents were present during the interviews with children to add a supportive factor. Of course, parents did not interfere in their children's responses and only encouraged them to respond.

Results

After analyzing the data, four main overarching themes were found. These themes framed and expressed the Czech preschool children's perception and consumption of the media content, their consumer behavior, and also their impact on family consumer behavior. Several sub-themes were extracted from main themes. These themes and their descriptions are summarized next. Sub-themes and relationships among them are also shown in Table 1.1.

Table 1.1 Themes, sub-themes, and interview examples

Themes	Sub-themes	Examples of participants' answers
Media, media format, and media content choice of preschool children	Print and electronic mass media (used for fairy tales, playing games, and educational programs)	"I let [my son] play a game on DVD as a reward, but at longest 30 minutes" (a mother)
		"My daughter most often watches programs on CT: D channel" (a mother)
Ritualization of the media consumption processes in preschool children	Consumption of media during meals Consumption of media after kindergarten Consumption of media before bedtime Consumption of media over the weekend	"After I have watched a cartoon on TV, we go for a walk" (a girl) "My daughter watches TV with her older brother and she especially watches the channel D" (a mother)

(Continued)

Table 1.1 (Continued)

Themes	Sub-themes	Examples of participants' answers
Identification of advertising appeals within the media content in preschool children	Distinction between advertising and other media Understanding persuasion of advertising	"Advertising is when for example for people to buy something in the store, or for sort of fairy tales" (a girl) "When I grow up, I will buy the bra I saw in my mom's magazine" (a girl)
Influence of media on shopping behavior of preschool children	Products for personal consumptions (such as toys or food) Products for consumption by all members of family (such as drugstore goods)	"I bought my daughter a Little Mole toy, Ariel (a washing gel), and a trampoline" (a mother)

Theme 1. Media, media format, and media content choice of preschool children

Children used electronic media mostly for watching stories and playing games. Gender differentiation was not seen in amount of time spent on the media, but there was gender differentiation in the selection of media contents that could be due to gender identification. Both girls and boys watched the educational TV programs that broadcast through the children's TV channel, a very popular medium for children and their parents.

Theme 2. Ritualization of the media consumption processes in preschool children

Media was a part of routine family life. It was used after coming home from kindergarten, during dinner, having snacks, and before going to bed. In addition to TV, other mentioned sources of media were DVDs and tablets. Television was the most frequently used medium so that it structured family time, especially during the weekends. Older siblings, as the models for their younger brothers and sisters, played the role of mediators and initiated the contact with the particular medium.

Theme 3. Identification of advertising appeals within the media content in preschool children

Preschool children could identify advertising products in media. For example, a mother said that her daughter could recognize that an advertised beverage was the beer her father drank. Older preschool children (5 to 7 years of age) considered advertising a persuasive tool for shopping. Advertising of products targeting adults were not understandable for children and they asked their parents about them. Moreover, children preferred witty advertising or advertising containing animated characters (preferably cartoons) or child actors. Children also related promoted products with their desires for their adulthood.

Theme 4. Influence of media on shopping behavior of preschool children

Buying preferences of children were influenced by media. Children pressured their parents in their shopping process. Such pressures increased with the children's age and were often accompanied by aggressive behaviors. Children influenced shopping behavior of the family with products designed for both their consumption and the consumption of other members of the family (Sramova & Pavelka, 2017).

2 Advertising targeting children

Children-directed marketing expenditures are spent on 20 separate promotional activity categories: television; radio; and print advertising; company websites; other internet advertising; packaging and labeling; advertising in movie theaters/videos/video games; other digital advertising (such as email and text messaging); in-store marketing; premium distribution; public entertainment events; product placement; character licensing/cross-promotions/ toy co-branding; sponsorship of sports teams or athletes; word-of-mouth marketing; viral marketing; celebrity endorsements; in-school marketing; advertising in conjunction with philanthropic endeavors; and other promotional activities. The reported expenditure of only 44 companies on food marketing directed to children under 12 was approximately $870 million in the U.S. in 2006.

Food and beverage products are heavily marketed to children and youth. Since children have gained increased purchasing power and influence on family purchase decisions, industries pay more attention to and invest more creativity and resources in the production and marketing of food and beverages for this target market. In recent years, the growth rate for food and beverage products targeted to children and youth was greater than the growth rate for food and beverage products targeted to the general market. And the majority of these food and beverage products were branded products with high total calories, sugar, salt, and fat, and low nutrients.

Historical review of marketing to children

Important changes in consumer society have historically involved new forms of triangulation; marketers allied with one group to reach their target market. One such shift occurred a century ago as women and merchants formed an alliance to overcome opposition to the emerging consumer economy from frugal, conservative husbands. Based on the belief that mothers' main concern was their children's health and well-being, marketers targeted mothers to reach children. But this pattern has changed. Today, the partnership is between children and marketers, who are sometimes implicitly, and sometimes explicitly, allied against parents. The gatekeeper model has become an archaic remnant of another era, operating only in the market for very young children. Advertisers have direct access to kids because they watch television without their parents. Marketers have also pried open other parent-free environments, most notably schools and the internet, where they speak directly to their target market. Indeed, marketers are connecting with children in an increasingly close embrace that parents find difficult to penetrate. This is even affecting how kids and parents get along.

The developing child, 1910s–1950s

Children were considered and treated as consumers even before there was any research to systematize knowledge about their commercial behavior and desires. In the first decades of the twentieth century in the U.S., there were niche markets for children's books, toys, furniture, and nursery ware, and a growing industry of ready-made clothing for all ages of youth. To build the children's world, many practitioners such as retailers, store buyers, manufacturers, and advertisers observed and attended to reports about the behavior of mothers and children. This personal observation and storytelling about consumers or consumer behavior performed a function similar to market research for retailers and manufacturers. By expanding the market for children's goods and changing the social position of children in an increasingly urban, diverse, and expanding social order in the interwar period, new kinds of knowledge came to exist about 'who children are' and how they were said to think and act at various ages. During the 1920s and 1930s, child psychology rose in public popularity and was a prominent feature in advice columns in parenting and child publications. As a result, manufacturers and advertisers could frame and produce goods in terms of scientific theories of children's growth and needs. Child development theories provided a template for early marketers in order to translate children's changing age-sensitive abilities into commercial action. In the 1940s, Grumbine proposed six age stages from age 2 to 18 and explained that how particular goods and promotions fit with the characteristics found in particular age ranges.

The desiring child, 1950s–1970s

The publication of *Advertising and Marketing to Young People* by Eugene Gilbert was proof of a cultural shift in attitudes toward the relationship between children, youth, and the consumer marketplace in the 1950s. To understand children's minds, Gilbert used psychological literature. But rather than considering simple phases in the developmental sequence or the educational value of a product, he emphasized children's desires and unique ability as key elements in determining which goods and promotions were appropriate for children. Considering the importance of children's desires marked a shift in the conceptualization of the child consumer as a part of a larger cultural change in the social understanding of children. Acknowledging children's wants and desires alongside those of adults caused commercial approaches to children to emerge. In the mid-1960s, a few efforts were undertaken to understand children's knowledge of and preferences for goods via direct interviews with children. In other words, through using these direct methods, consumer researchers were looking for understanding of how children perceived the commercial world and how they experienced it. However, the focus on children's knowledge and perspectives did not replace developmental and psychological models but tended to accompany and supplement them.

The rise of the knowing, active child

According to developmental psychology, children's actions and thoughts progress through a series of stages. Until the 1990s, developmental psychology dominated approaches to studying childhood, including research on consumer behavior. But in that decade, a significant epistemological break took hold in the understanding of children and childhood. A new approach to childhood had moorings within and outside of studies of consumption and consumer life. The United Nations Convention on the Rights of the Child (UNCRC), adopted in 1989 as an agreement among most nations, is a human rights treaty which sets out the civil, political, economic, social, health, and cultural rights of children. In the late 1980s and early 1990s, sociology and anthropology were regarded as the new approach to children and childhood. Childhood, as Prout and James argued, was not reducible to other social variables or institutions like the economy, polity, or biology and hence it made no sense to discuss the child as a stand-alone idea apart from culture, economy, and history.

Children's market research and the new child consumer in the 1990s and beyond

In the 1980s, in a strong economic environment and a favorable social-moral climate, market practitioners focused on devising and applying various research techniques to identify children's understandings of and feelings about consumer goods and promotional activities. Discovering the child's perspective became a gold standard to surviving in a market that relied on children's tastes and preferences. In the 1980s and 1990s, marketers faced a puzzle. Despite increasing sales of children's products, there were few ways to confidently measure children's direct role in their own and their family's purchase decisions. It was also unknown how investing in brands and products at one point in time would convert into future sales and loyal customers. The children themselves also infused a measure of uncertainty. Children's reputation as fickle and easily influenced increased worries about the robustness of the children's market, especially outside traditionally successful areas such as toys, cartoons, candy, and fast foods. In the early 1990s, some published books about the strength and possibilities of the children's market focused on the promise of qualitative research. New techniques such as role-playing with children, picture drawing by children, focus groups, interviews, observation of children playing, or observation of parents and children in retail stores were used to enter into the children's world.

In the late 1990s and early 2000s, a number of market research companies entered the children's knowledge market and some advertising agencies added their own research divisions devoted exclusively to children. The children's perspective itself became a valuable product. The connection between the consumer market and children's selves had been deeply penetrated and marketers went beyond simply satisfying children's desires or answering a need; they began to empower children. Qualitative market research on children became an essential part of marketing decisions because it introduced a conception of the child as a knowing, active being in the here and now. There are still issues surrounding the developmental appropriateness of marketing and advertising, but these issues have changed in response to the rising contemporary cultural dominance of the child customer.

Advertising according to James, Prout, and Jenks' perspective on childhood

James, Prout, and Jenks divide the perspectives on childhood into Pre-Sociological and Sociological (Table 2.1).

The 'evil child' needs shielding from the urgings of advertising because of his or her proneness to wickedness. According to 'innocent child' perspective, resistance to the commercialization of children is necessary so that Monbiot stated that children's advertising is the marketing of insecurity and generates self-consciousness among the only group of people who have been free from it. Children are less experienced and more impressionable than adults and therefore need protection against harmful media content of all sorts. Objecting to advertising to children can be a form of political substitution for objecting to advertising in general. An 'unconscious

Table 2.1 James, Prout, and Jenks' categorization of childhood

Pre-Sociological child	Sociological child
Evil child: prone to wickedness	Socially constructed child: denies essential forms or constraints on childhood
Innocent child: naturally good	
Immanent child: neither good nor bad	Tribal child: treats children on their own terms and worlds
Naturally developing child: based on developmental psychology	Minority group child: recognizes the disservice done to children by social convention
The unconscious child: in the context of psychoanalysis	Social structural child: defines childhood by the common space occupied by children in the structures of societies

Source: Adapted from O'Sullivan (2005).

child' can make adults anxious. It means that the unruly and destructive 'id', whose desires are motivated by marketing and advertising activities, threaten adults' autonomy and self-determination. So, adults will be protected through protecting children from advertising. In this way, adults will be protected from the pestering of the external 'evil child', and/or from the more insidious demands of the internal 'unconscious child'.

According to 'the naturally developing child' perspective, children's understanding of advertising depends on their natural development. Removing advertising may be prejudicial to children's welfare by removing an important source of consumer socialization. Based on Piaget's cognitive development theory, preoperational children are unaware of perspectives on the world other than their own. Due to immediate perceptions, preoperational children accept an advertisement as a kind of public information broadcast. Concrete operational children's thinking is more structured than preoperationals' and they are capable of understanding that the world is not always as it appears. So, they become aware of the persuasive intent of advertising. Advertisers use cognitive psychology to justify their activities because it represents the most ethically respectable version of the way advertising works. According to the cognitive development approach, people think about their decisions before they make them. Thus, advertising only offers some ideas and information, and people themselves process and evaluate these offers and information in order to make rational choices. Such a cognitive view considered children as young consumers who are interested in making choices and needing information about them.

Contrary to cognitive psychology, behaviorism believes less in people's intelligence. Behaviorists argue that people react to stimuli rather than evaluating information. Advertising manipulates people and advertisers can elicit the required reaction by offering the appropriate cue. Consistent with the discussion of the 'unconscious child', behaviorism effectively dissolves the difference between adults and children, making everybody susceptible to unscrupulous string-pullers. This is the reason that research that focuses on cognitive processes is attractive for advertisers. Research that relied on cognitive development theories presents some methodological problems. For example, researchers may underestimate younger children's actual appreciation of the meaning and intention of advertising because of their lack of linguistic facility. Using a nonverbal response mechanism was Donohue et al.'s solution for this problem.

Childhood sociology was established as a field within the oppositional dichotomies of modernist sociology during the 1990s with the aim of creating a space for childhood in sociological discourse. Childhood sociology criticized former child sociologists and developmental psychologists for their top-down approach to children. This approach considers children and childhood as social and cultural constructs and active agents at all levels in society. The 'tribal child', as a sociological perspective, emerged from qualitative research traditions such as the classic ethnography of Opie and Opie, which established a picture of children on their own terms. This perspective emphasizes children's own roles in constructing their childhoods and gives a more active account of childhood than its alternative, namely 'socially-constructed child'. It is also more fully dimensional than the 'minority group child' and similar to 'social-structural child' in that it emphasizes the self-sufficiency of the world of childhood. For the 'tribal child', television watching in general is part of a culture that adults can only guess at, unless they want to start listening to children more seriously in their research.

According to Alan Prout's recent argument, childhood sociology now needs to be revised and move beyond dichotomies such as child-adult, agent-structure, individual-society, and being-becoming.

The persistent effect of childhood advertising exposure

Elementary school age is considered the best age to educate, change, and modify eating habits. Although children's consumer behavior continues to develop during adolescence and adulthood, children have become acquainted with all aspects of their consumer behavior by the end of elementary school period, at least in a rudimentary form. According to cognitive psychology, what is learned early is learned well. People recognize words, objects, faces, and brand names they have learned early in life more quickly and more accurately than those acquired later in life; possibly because early acquired concepts are more firmly embedded in semantic memory than later acquired concepts. Moreover, it is argued that early acquired concepts shape neural networks into an efficient form for representing them so that this structure resists attempts at reconfiguration by later learned concepts. As a result, what children learn from advertising may be particularly accessible in adulthood. As Ellis et al. argued, this age-of-acquisition effect gives some benefits to brands that target consumers at an early age that make them more memorable.

People's ability to cope with advertising increases through skills and knowledge acquired during childhood and adolescence. Before fully developing such skills and knowledge, children are not skeptical about advertising and are likely to develop affect-laden knowledge structures for advertised products. Also, the associations learned and made earlier in life are more easily accessible in adulthood than those learned later. Thus, how a person deals with advertising throughout the lifetime can be a function of his or her extant abilities at the time of initial encoding of advertising into memory in childhood.

TV advertising targeting children

Young believed that children realize that there is a source (supplier) to create advertising and its aim is to persuade the audience to purchase. But the history of advertising aimed at children extends far before this view to children's understanding of TV advertising. In the mid-1950s, the television network ABC and Disney collaboratively set the foundations for children's television. As they had not discovered the value of the children's market, their efforts were limited to influencing families' purchasing behavior. In that time, the main concern of advertising was to persuade the target audience to see the benefits of consumption of the advertised product. Toys with unknown brands became popular after appearing on television advertising. Over the following 15 to 20 years, this evolutionary process led to the creation of a new industry of children's television advertising.

Since children were considered easily influenced targets who were incapable of perceiving the persuasive intent of advertising, this newly emerging industry was criticized and discussion of protecting children from advertising was broached.

In order to understand how children process advertising information, the nature of advertising to children should be examined. Advertisers usually used fun and happy appeals in order to direct children toward aspects of advertising messages related to positive affect. When children perceive positive affect, they need fewer processing resources that lead to affect-congruent evaluations and reach judgments more rapidly. In fact, positive affect offers short-term rewards over long-term consequences and changes brand beliefs. Coupling such positive affect with underdeveloped advertising knowledge can increase the probability of biased product evaluations. Due to involvement with fun and happiness aspects of advertising, it is expected that children do not consider advertiser's persuasive intent or do not integrate their understandings of such intent with multiple product dimensions when they are processing advertising messages.

As children grow up, they will understand who pays for the advertising, who makes the ads (and why), why the ads are broadcast on certain channels, and so on. Many studies indicate that children gradually acquire the ability to distinguish television programs from commercials. Of course, the position of the commercial within the program also acts as a moderator variable in such distinguishing. Since children, as their ages increase, understand advertising's persuasive intent and also use alternative sources of information, they depend less on television advertising and are not as easily convinced.

Research sample

Title

A new scale to assess children's attitude toward TV advertising.

Objective

There are limitations concerning the predictive power of children's general attitude toward advertising. Despite such limitations, understanding children's attitude toward advertising, its determinants, and the way to measure it is still needed. In this regard, some attempts have been made in the past, but they did not propose the scales with fully assessed validity. Therefore, a new investigation of children's attitude toward advertising seems necessary, especially in the current era where children have obtained more power in the consumption area and have been surrounded by advertising targeting children. Developing such a scale is of paramount importance to both practitioners and those responsible for advertising control and should be employed before exposing children to particular advertisements. Accordingly, this study developed and validated a scale measuring children's global attitude toward TV advertising.

Method

This study followed the different steps of Churchill's paradigm (detailed in Figure 2.1) with the purpose of developing a scale to measure children's attitude toward TV advertising. Participating in the study were 714 children aged 8 to 12 from a European, French-speaking country. Data were collected in class (about 20 children at a time) in order to be assured that children worked individually. The study did not provide any report on how principles of studies involving children were respected.

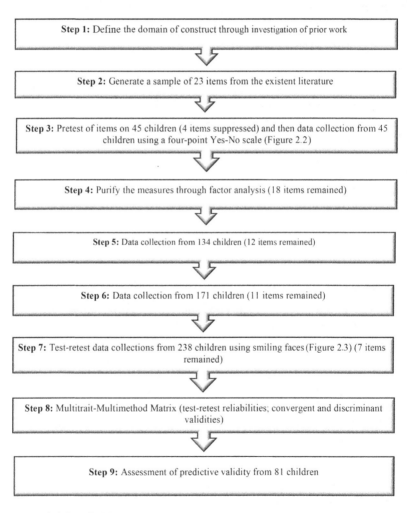

Figure 2.1 Detailed framework

Source: Adapted from Derbaix and Pecheux (2003).

Results

The final scale was a 7-item one (Figure 2.4). As is logical, more abstract or latent constructs needed more items to be measured. Five items out of seven were related to entertainment and other two items were related to credibility. Therefore, the backbone of children's attitude toward TV advertising was entertainment (Derbaix & Pecheux, 2003).

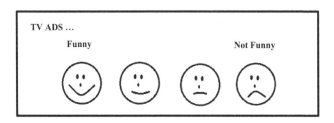

I like advertisements

NO	no	yes	YES
☐	☐	☐	☐

Figure 2.2 Four-point Yes-No scale, used for step 3

TV ADS ...

Funny   **Not Funny**

Figure 2.3 Alternative scale – smiling faces format used for step 7

I believe what they show in TV advertisements (Credibility dimension)
NO ☐   no ☐   yes ☐   **YES** ☐

I like TV advertisements (Entertaining dimension)
NO ☐   no ☐   yes ☐   **YES** ☐

I think TV advertisements are great (Entertaining dimension)
NO ☐   no ☐   yes ☐   **YES** ☐

When commercials are aired on TV, I feel like watching them (Entertaining dimension)
NO ☐   no ☐   yes ☐   **YES** ☐

I think TV advertisements are good (Entertaining dimension)
NO ☐   no ☐   yes ☐   **YES** ☐

I think TV advertisements tell the truth (Credibility dimension)
NO ☐   no ☐   yes ☐   **YES** ☐

When commercials are aired on TV, I enjoy watching them (Entertaining dimension)
NO ☐   no ☐   yes ☐   **YES** ☐

Figure 2.4 Final scale

3 Advertising and food choice

The process of food choice is guided by a number of mechanisms that are fundamentally different and that can interact with each other. Factors determining consumer food choice are clearly of interest not only to governments, industries, and consumers themselves, but also to psychologists, sociologists, anthropologists, market researchers, and other analysts of contemporary society. Key questions associated with understanding food choice, such as 'who eats what and why?', can be asked from within the perspective of a multitude of different disciplines, and it is essential that these different disciplines interact if these questions are to be answered in any systematic and definitive way.

Food plays a central role in family life and food choice is one of the areas where children are said to have gained major influence. Moreover, species that can live in many different types of environments, and have a varied diet are considered generalists. 'To eat or not to eat' is an often made, but weighty decision. Good food means life, and bad food may mean death. Over recent years, social marketing campaigns that focus upon healthy eating have become commonplace all over the world. Given the social and individual costs of the increasing rates of overweightness and obesity, understanding food choice from a consumer behavior perspective may offer insights that enhance the effectiveness of healthy eating intervention strategies, especially those focused on youth. The concern with the younger consumer stems from research that tells if an unhealthy food choice pattern develops during young adulthood, it likely will continue for the rest of the person's life.

Based on ecological systems theory (EST), behavioral patterns are the outcome of an interaction between the developing person and her or his environment. In order to identify the factors that affect human development, EST considers both the individual's immmediate environment and the interrelated factors which may not involve individuals directly but still impact them. Accordingly, food choice as a behavioral pattern can be influenced by personal and environmental factors.

Marketing mix and food choice

According to the American Marketing Association (AMA) definition, marketing is the process of planning and executing the conception, pricing, promotion, and distribution of goods, services, and ideas to create exchanges that satisfy individual and organizational objectives. There are many definitions of marketing, but most of them have a common core, namely exchanges. Thus, marketing could be defined as any effort aimed at increasing sales of a particular product or service. To accomplish this aim, marketers should decide about marketing parameters – those parameters controlled by the seller that will have an impact on a potential buyer's probability of actually buying. The most well-known typology of marketing parameters is still the famous 4 Ps, including product, price, place (distribution), and promotion (marketing communication). In food marketing, similarly, marketing parameters are parameters in the hands of the seller with a probable impact on buying a certain food item by a potential consumer.

Products, product quality, and branding

In the food industry, exchange can simply be realized by the physical product; something that can be prepared and eaten. In food marketing, as everywhere else, the starting point of business activities is analyzing the various consumers' needs fulfilled by eating. In the other words, in order to increase the likelihood of success of new products, food product development should be built on a thorough understanding of consumer needs and food choice that means consumer-led product development or market-oriented product development. Food quality, as an element of parameter of product, is a reciprocal relationship between consumers and products. For consumers, quality is all that they want to get out of the product. Perceived quality is traded off against price and other costs to determine food choice. On the other hand, for food producers, it is necessary to translate consumers' perceived quality into technical characteristics of the product. Consumers usually consider four major aspects for food quality including sensory quality (sensory evaluation entailing taste, smell, appearance, and texture, considered the most central quality aspect), health (in terms of nutrition and safety), convenience (in preparation, buying, storing, eating, and disposing of food), and certain process characteristics (such as organic production, animal welfare, and being free of genetically modified organisms (GMOs)).

Quality dimensions are also categorized into search, experience, and credence dimensions. Search dimensions are those where the quality can be ascertained by the buyer at the time of purchase (e.g. the appearance of an apple). Experience dimensions are those where the quality can be ascertained only after the purchase (e.g. the taste of an apple). Finally, credence dimensions are those where the average consumer him- or herself can never ascertain the quality, but has to trust the judgement of others (like whether the apple is healthy or organically produced). Consumers usually form expectations about the quality because most aspects of the quality of a product are unknown to them at the time of purchase. They form these expectations based on quality cues including intrinsic cues and extrinsic cues. Intrinsic cues can be part of the physical product, such as the expected taste and tenderness of a piece of meat from its visible fat and from its color. Some examples of extrinsic cues are the shop in which the product is being bought, the price of the product, and of course, the advertising of the product. Packaging, as a part of the physical product, also adds extra quality to the product. Packaging as an element of product parameter, is a carrier of information that may provide cues which consumers use to infer the quality of the product. It provides additional possibilities for storage and serving and helps protect the food product while taking it home.

Brand name, as another element of product parameter, helps consumers when they are choosing between competing items. So the brand's presence or absence is considered as a very important informational cue. The presence of a well-established brand on the label can influence consumers' choice through influencing their sensory expectations. Brands, as a very important quality cue, can be used to signal superior quality to consumers. Brands as the signals for superior quality can have a strong impact on consumer food choice, and brand equity will be reached when consumers become brand loyal. A particularly intriguing development in the food sector is the increasing share of food retail shops' own brands of food. Retailers could substitute the low sales of a large number of less important brands by using their own brand. The position of a retailers' own brands, which began with the aim of price competition, is shifting to quality competition.

Persuasion and market communication

There are numerous stimuli that compete together in order to persuade consumers to buy or not to buy certain food products. Some of these stimuli are in control of marketers, whereas others are not marketer controlled. Marketers can design, control, or change marketing communication measures including advertising, labels, in-store communication, personal selling, publicity, and sponsoring (a hybrid of advertising and publicity). In the food area, consumers rarely allocate much effort to get information about new food products or their characteristics. Therefore, the vast majority of market communication effects occur in situations of accidental exposure, which increases the likelihood that the information is never consciously perceived by consumers. Inother words, marketers are experiencing marketing clutter: a marketplace overcrowded with products, leading to huge competition for customers' conscious attention.

There are vast discussions and debates about the impact of advertising on food choice. The main reason for this is the worldwide prevalence of obesity and its link to food advertising, especially that directed at children. In this regard, the public health nutrition movement aims at controlling and even banning unfettered advertising that is known as a means of promoting unhealthy eating practices.

Price perception and price impact

The parameter of price affects consumer food choice in at least two different ways: it relates the product to the consumer's economic means and indicates what the consumer has to sacrifice in order to obtain the product, and it is used as indicator of quality that may enter consumer decision making as a heuristic in different ways. To process price information (Figure 3.1), after

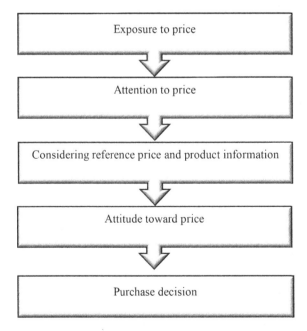

Figure 3.1 Price information processing
Source: Adapted from Grunert (2006).

perceiving price, consumers try to form an opinion on whether the price is favorable or not; this is called attitude towards the price. This process usually involves comparing the perceived price to some kind of benchmark price, which is termed the reference price. Helson, through adaptation level theory, explains that the reference price is formed as a weighted average of previously perceived prices of the same product. Also, the maximum price a consumer is willing to pay for a given product is called the willingness to pay (WTP), which may be higher than the actual market price for a consumer who has bought the product, and can be anything between zero and the market price for those who have not bought the product.

Distribution channels and modes of shopping

There are various ways to distribute food products to consumers. Food products are usually distributed via supermarkets and hypermarkets. Although physical shops have been on the decline for many years, they occasionally grow in certain niche areas, often when integrated into bigger shopping malls. Farm-gate purchasing and box schemes are popular in the area of organic produce. Internet purchasing, which only works for some specialized areas like wine, has not yet had breakthrough success. A reason for this can be the importance of sensory quality in the process of food choice.

Based on Russel and Mehrabian's environmental psychology approach to retailing, the store environment is characterized by two dimensions: sense modality variables that deal with elements like color and temperature, and information rate, which deals with the quantity of information drawn from the store environment per unit of time. Depending on the interaction of the two environmental variables and consumers' personality, the store environment leads to emotional reactions and corresponding approach-avoidance behaviors by consumers.

The psychology of food advertising

The common aims of advertising are retaining existing users of a product or behavior; encouraging users of other similar products to switch to the advertised product; and enticing new users to purchase the advertised products. The advertising industry aimed at children claims that the function of advertising, as a means of communication, is to encourage children to switch brands, not to eat greater quantities from a wide range of products. Advertising works through two psychological avenues called central and peripheral routes. Based on the elaboration likelihood model's (ELM) assumption, people take the central route to persuasion under conditions of high involvement, and they take a peripheral route under conditions of low involvement. The central route to persuasion, which is often used by public health nutrition and social marketing campaigns, is taken by consumers when there is a rational appeal on the basis of factual information. When a public health nutrition campaign uses appeals to healthy eating behavior on the principle of danger or damage to health, indeed it is encouraging people to healthy behaviors through activating a logical thought process. The central route to persuasion involves the standard hierarchy of effects (i.e. cognition, affect, behavior). In contrast, the peripheral route is taken when there is not enough motivation to think about the marketer's arguments, and instead people are likely to use other cues to decide how to react to the message. Peripheral routes to persuasion are the favorite approach for food and advertising industries and usually use exposure and reinforcement of cultural norms to influence behavior. This approach is more to do with the values, images, branding, value for money, and social values surrounding the food rather than the food itself. In theory, central routes are known to be more effective and less expensive than peripheral routes, but in practice, peripheral routes seem to be more efficient. A reason is that the central route to persuasion relies on the individual making decisions based on cognitive processes, while the peripheral route to persuasion directly taps into behavior via impulses.

When consumers are involved with a subject, it is not easy to influence or change their attitude. It is also not easy asking or persuading consumers to adopt new behaviors or quit existing ones. For example, it would be easier to convince those who already eat fruit to eat more fruit than to persuade those who do not eat fruit to begin such diet. To have a big picture, it should be considered that advertising is only part of the whole marketing process and does not work effectively if the other dimension of marketing process, namely distribution, acts weakly. In other words, when a new brand of food product is advertised, it is essential that it appears at the point of demand: when and where consumers demand it. Although public health advertising campaigns can be very effective in increasing knowledge, influencing attitudes, and even creating demand, they ultimately fail if they have not been accompanied with a strong distribution system by which an individual can access the product or change behavior with minimum disruption. In the model of planning for advertising, there is a hierarchy of effect that is based on the three interrelated processes of learning (cognition); feeling (affect); and doing (behavior). The central persuasion process described earlier starts with learning (cognition/logic), leads to feeling (affective processes), and then leads to behavior.

Table 3.1 Psychological processes in advertising showing the type of engagement

	Think	*Feel*
High involvement	Logical Cognition → affect → behavior (Learn feel do)	Affective Affect → cognition → behavior (Feel learn do)
Low involvement	Habitual Behavior → cognition → affect (Do learn feel)	Satisfaction Behavior → affect → cognition (Do feel learn)

Source: Adapted from Caraher and Landon (2006).

The role of children in family food choice based on consumer socialization

John believed that the family is the main socialization agent for young children. Parents train children for consumer skills (direct influence), play the role as models of consumer behavior (indirect influence), and supervise children's consumer opportunities. They also influence children's cognitive abilities and motivate them to use such abilities in consumer situations. Overall, socialization factors such as parents, media, and the school influence children's behavior and form their knowledge about consumption. Parents teach children how to become consumers through transmitting consumption skills, knowledge, tastes, and preferences so that children have to be inducted into a system of consuming. This approach, which comes from traditional research protocols (such as the parental influence), considers children as passive members in family decision-making processes. John believed that consumption theories are not appropriate for children because they do not know childhood and have failed to account for the place, practices, and existence of children in consumer decision-making processes. In this sense, children's voices are not accounted for in the literature on family food-decision-making processes.

Contrary to the parental influence perspective about children's consumption, consumer socialization can also occur in a reverse direction, from children to parents, rather than be unidirectional. Children can play the role as socialization agents and actively change their parents' beliefs. Therefore, consumer socialization occurs in both directions between parents and children.

Advertising, nutritional beliefs, and food choice

Childhood obesity is a growing problem in many countries. Meanwhile, the questionable impact of food marketing on children's obesity has provoked a considerable interest in food marketing aimed at children. Food marketing, as a multi-billion-dollar industry, influences children's food preferences and consumption through promoting high fat, salt, and sugar (HFSS) foods to children, while these foods put children's health at risk. Concerns about the possible effects of food advertising have been fueled by empirical evidence that children's exposure to advertising may indeed affect their consumption patterns. On the other hand, the food and advertising industry groups, despite the aforementioned facts, claim that there is not enough evidence of a relationship between unhealthy food advertising and children's obesity and health status. In order to support this claim, they argue that there are not enough longitudinal studies that could prospectively link children's exposure to food advertising and their nutrition and weight outcomes.

Children start to solidify their analytical, logical, and rational judgment around 7 or 8 years old. At these ages, they are able to retain and process information from a more self-reflective perspective. Children usually have good nutritional understanding and knowledge, but they do not tend to select foods in alignment with their knowledge. One reason is that they are easily influenced or manipulated by what they see or experience. Thus, along with parents and schools' effects, advertising can contribute to children's nutritional beliefs and consumption patterns.

The food industry contributes to childhood obesity through the promotion of energy-dense food directed to children. A food content analysis of popular children websites shows that the most marketed food products are candy, cereal, quick-service restaurant meals, and snacks. Consequently, children's food decisions are often made in high-calorie or nutrient-poor environments. Repeated exposure to marketing communication has an impact on children's food choice and preferences through building awareness, reinforcing food familiarity, reducing neophobia (fear of trying new foods), and enhancing consumption. The advertised foods include the dietary pattern associated with increased risk of obesity and dental caries in childhood and are also in conflict with health authority recommendations to encourage children and adolescents to eat a wide variety of nutritious foods and limit consumption of foods containing high amounts of fat and sugar. Evidence is accumulating on food advertising influences on children's nutrition knowledge, food preferences, purchasing requests, and diet quality.

Nevertheless, food marketing and especially advertising has potential power over the prevention of obesity through changing attitudes, preferences, and behaviors. The most recent studies exploring the relationship between food marketing and children's diet-related outcomes found an association between food advertising and children's food knowledge, attitudes, preferences, behaviors, and health status. Thus, more responsible food marketing may improve children's health, although there are different opinions about what counts as responsible marketing.

As was discussed earlier, children's most common information sources about food health and attitude towards food are, respectively, parents, school, and media. Media research on other health issues indicates that counter-advertising can be an effective strategy for promoting healthy behavior (see Chapter 5). In an experimental study, Dixon et al. found that advertising for nutritious foods promotes positive attitudes and beliefs concerning these foods. Pempek and Calvert's (in the U.S.) and Dias and Agante's (in Australia) experimental studies also showed that children tend to choose according to what was being advertised in a game. Children who played the healthier version of the advergame selected and ate significantly more healthy snacks than did those who played the less healthy version. These findings state that advergames could be a powerful tool to healthy advertising.

Research sample

Title

Television use and children's food choices: qualitative approach.

Objective

Todays' children's dietary patterns are influenced by unhealthy food preferences and contain high intakes of fat, saturated fat, and refined carbohydrates and low intakes of fruit, vegetables, and complex carbohydrates. Therefore, children are at increasing risk of heart disease, certain cancers, diabetes, hypertension, and obesity. Excessive TV viewing during childhood plays an important role in these risky dietary patterns. Food is the most frequently advertised product category on children's TV programming. The results of a large body of research have verified that children can be very sensitive to the effects of advertising and exposure to food advertising effectively promotes their consumption of the advertised food. The present pilot study, which was exploratory in nature, aimed at obtaining preliminary data about the as yet unknown relationship between TV use and children's food choice in Brazil.

Method

An exploratory study was conducted with the purpose of identifying the relationship between TV use and children's food choice using a qualitative approach. Data were collected through 12 focus groups. Each focus group interview was conducted within the school setting using open-ended questions to ensure consistency in interviewing style (Figure 3.2). Moreover, a semi-structured questioning route was used to allow for some flexibility

– Can a food be healthy and tasty at the same time? Give examples.
– Do you like eating fruits? How often?
– What about vegetables?
– Do you like eating snack foods? How often?
– What else do you like to eat?
– Do your parents try to interfere with your eating habits?
– When you have your own money to spend, what food items do you buy?
– Do you like watching TV? When?
– What are your favorite shows?
– Do you usually eat something while watching TV?
– Do your parents try to interfere with your TV viewing habits?
– Between watching TV and playing outside, what do you prefer?
– Do you practice any sports?

Figure 3.2 Focus group interview structure: sample of main questions

in accordance with the topics. Each focus group interview lasted approximately 30 minutes and was audio recorded (after participants' permission) for later transcription. A total of 57 students aged 7 to 10 years old participated in the study. The majority of the students were white and from middle-class families living near the school. Participants were divided into groups based on their grade and gender (range of 4–6 students in each focus group). Since there were not enough participants to create just female or male groups, some groups contained both genders.

To analyze the data, content analysis was used. First, the ideas or trends were coded in the transcript margin; then, codes were selectively retrieved and reassembled together, and finally, themes were built through grouping the categories of previous stage. During the coding process, the context of responses was considered in terms of the stimulus that elicited each response. To observe the principles of studies involving children, child participants returned the consent forms signed by their parents.

Results

After the systematic process was completed, the data were categorized as five themes (Table 3.2).

Table 3.2 Themes, descriptions, and interview examples

Themes	Description	Examples of participants' answers
Consumption of fruits, vegetables, and snack foods	Most participants had positive remarks about fruit and vegetable consumption that showed a regular intake of salads and fresh fruits. However, a few students had negative comments on consumption of fruits and vegetables. Also, many children admitted liking and eating snack foods more than they should.	"Every day I eat three fruits: one in the morning, other at noon and another one at night." "I don't really eat them; I just suck the juice and throw away the rest."
Parental interference over food choices	Parents controlled their children's food choice in several ways, including not buying their children's food requests; restricting their children to access to some food items at home; educating, negotiating, or forcing children to eat some foods; or appealing for health reasons.	"My mother warned me that if I did not eat the vegetables in my plate I would stay all day long eating what was left from my lunch . . . then I started to eat vegetables."
Food consumer behavior	Most participants had money to spend as allowance or pocket money. When they were allowed to choose food items, they usually spent their money on snack foods such as sweet and salted snacks, candy, gum, lollipops, and ice pops.	"I sneak to the supermarket and buy a lot of stuff . . . Tic Tacs."
TV viewing habits	Participants watched TV daily, at all hours, especially during meals and at night. Some of them were passionate about it, while watching TV was reported as the last resort for some others. A common habit in the participants was eating food during TV viewing. According to children's reports, eating in front of the TV set influenced the amount of food they ate; some ate more while some others forgot to eat.	"I will watch anything that is on TV."

Themes	Description	Examples of participants' answers
Physical activity	Although TV viewing influenced children's food behavior, it did not keep them from being physically active. They reported doing active leisure activities at home or outside their apartments and also attending sport classes such as swimming, soccer, and dance.	"When it's a hot day and I am allowed to play, my friend goes to my place . . . or I go to his . . . ride our bikes."

Consistent with previous studies, this study proved that the children who were allowed to watch TV at all hours, apparently without any interference from the parents, were heavily exposed to unhealthy food advertising. These advertisements were accomplishing and reinforcing children's natural fondness for sweets and snacks, and influencing their purchases (Fiates, Amboni, & Teixeira, 2008).

4 Stereotyping and advertising characters/mascots

Stereotyping and prejudice may work through two distinct processes called controlled and automatic. When the individual is aware of the process and has the time and the capacity to control or alter his or her responses, he or she is acting based on controlled or conscious processing. In contrast, automatic processes require no conscious effort or attention, and occur without control. Stereotypical knowledge activated automatically can influence subsequent judgments. Devine believed that automatic and controlled processes in prejudice operate independently. In the other words, automatically activated stereotypes are independent of explicit attitudes toward the target group. Measuring stereotypes and prejudice (or any attitude) help with predicting behavior and recognizing the distinction between two discussed prejudices, which can be important in this regard.

There is the evidence that explicit attitudes are not good predictors of prejudicial behavior. However, there are some reasons that automatically activated knowledge can be a better predictor of behavior than explicitly reported attitudes. Due to social norms against expressing prejudice, people are usually reluctant to overtly admit negative attitudes or stereotypes. Moreover, people are almost unaware of their underlying attitudes and stereotypes, and therefore they cannot accurately report these attitudes. Finally, when conscious beliefs influence perceiver's behavior, then he or she has sufficient motivation to enact them. Exposure to a stereotype can lead to increases in stereotype-consistent behavior. For example, the shape or physique of cartoon characters or cartoon brand mascots – an increasingly prevalent phenomenon in children's programs (such as books, graphic novels, TV shows, movies, and video games) and advertising of products high in added sugars, salt, and fat for children – can lead children to choose and consume more unhealthy food (stereotype-consistent behavior) through activating the overweight stereotype.

Body build stereotypes

Physical appearance is about how one is perceived by oneself and by others. Indeed, physical appearance is represented by one's body. Stereotypes are defined as a set of beliefs about the personal attributes of a group of people. According to the results of studies on weight stereotypes, people usually associate more negative personality constructs with over- and under-weight body builds than with the average body build. Research also indicates that children are able to identify body build stereotypes around the age of 5 years old. Stereotypes become more multidimensional and consistent as age increases. Accordingly, stereotypic beliefs about body build will be increased as children grow up so that the perception of the overweight stereotype becomes more negative and the perception of the average stereotype becomes more positive.

Social learning theory can explain the relationship between body builds and perceived attributes. This theory states that a stereotype is developed both directly and indirectly. Socially reinforced values and cultural transmission could indirectly lead to a stereotype. A stereotype may also be developed by building relationships between behavior and body types through direct experience. Evolutionary biology also presents an alternative explanation for stereotypes. It explains that a stereotype could be the result of the natural process of developing prototypes of a category of people. Therefore, each prototype or stereotype distinguishes the average value of the attributes characteristic of that category and provides information for planning future interactions with the people of that category.

Prejudice against obese people

Obese people almost always experience stigma and discrimination. The term of 'civilized oppression', as it is called by Rogge et al., can be used to describe the pattern of ongoing, daily denigration and condemnation that obese persons experience. Weight bias is evident by age 5 and among people who believe that one's body size is controllable. Weight bias occurs in a dyadic context involving a perceiver and a target; cognitive and affective responses to targets that vary in weight are presumably shaped by socialization processes.

Jones et al. defined stigma as a mark that links a person to undesirable characteristics. Attribution theory provides the theoretical framework for why negative attributes are ascribed to obese individuals. For obesity, the negativity of attributes can be explained by the influence of causal beliefs and responsibility. Stigmatized conditions may be associated with other forms of marginalization, such as poverty, disability, or racial or cultural discrimination, resulting in the experience of layered stigma. In the other words, obese people usually experience a wide variety of negative feedback. They are seen as unattractive, aesthetically displeasing, morally and emotionally impaired, alienated from their sexuality, weak-willed, and unlikable by many groups such as thin people, health care workers, employers, peers, potential romantic partners, their parents, and even by themselves. In some societies such as the United States, obesity is associated with lower socioeconomic status. The reason may be the difficulties they experience in regard with advancement in the job force and higher education because of less support by their parents and generally by society. Obese students meet many obstacles such as harassment and rejection from peers at school, negative teacher attitudes, lower college acceptance rates, and wrongful dismissals from college. It is argued that there is weight prejudice even in preschool children, as the children may judge overweight classmates as undesirable playmates compared to average weight children. Research also shows that elementary school age children describe obese children as ugly, selfish, lazy, and stupid individuals that have few friends, lie, and get teased.

Some studies have also revealed that obese individuals may be at an intellectual disadvantage compared to non-obese persons. The association between obesity and lower intelligence can have some possible explanations. First, obese people may have real deficiencies in intellectual or work-related skills that cause poor performance in life activities such as education. Of course, little research supports this explanation. Another plausible explanation is that weight stigma in the form of prejudice or discrimination may cause deficiencies in obese individuals. Obese individuals may behave consistently with stereotypes based on self-fulfilling prophecies. They themselves even tend to express weight bias so that some overweight people have negative weight attitudes and apply negative stereotypes to themselves. Some documented harmful weight-based stereotypes are being lazy, weak-willed, unsuccessful, unintelligent, lacking self-discipline, and being noncompliant with weight-loss treatment, which leads to prejudice and discrimination against obese persons in multiple domains of living.

Theories of weight bias and stigmatization

Socialization theory

As socialization theory discusses, social and cultural factors could create an idealized and attractive body image in society and therefore shape weight bias. Socialization theory argues that weight bias and attitudes toward weight are learned in the social context. Socialization theory predicts that there are positive responses to thin bodies and negative responses to larger bodies. This means that weight bias should be linear; judgments are more negative when weight increases and are more positive when weight decreases. This theory has also predicted cultural differences in regard to weight.

Intergroup relations theory

There are implicit and explicit discrimination and bias against individuals who deviate from cultural norms – individuals such as members of a particular minority group, the physically disabled, or the mentally ill. Weight is a normally distributed variable in the general population and most people's weight is around the mean of weight in the population. Therefore, individuals who are an average weight may be considered an 'in-group' and thin or obese individuals may be considered an 'out-group'. Intergroup relations theory predicts more positive judgments of in-group members than out-group members. Contrary to socialization theory, intergroup relations theory predicts curvilinear weight bias, that is, when the target's weight increases or decreases, the perceiver's judgment should become more negative. In contrast to these predictions, most studies are on overweight bias and there is little attention to bias against thin people. In this sense, findings are rather complicated because society practically forces people to accept thinness as a beauty ideal. Advertising and other forms of media also convey that thinness is attractive.

Pathogen avoidance theory

Kurzban and Leary emphasized that stigmatization is a means for evolution. They argued that humans avoid members of different groups for survival and adaptation. When features of a type deviate from the average, it may be considered a signal that activates a brain mechanism to avoid infection or harm. Hence, stigmatization is a process that operates for survival purposes that involves the avoidance and exclusion of out-group members from social interaction, as the ability to detect and avoid infection allow the organism to produce healthy offspring. However, such prejudicial reactions (e.g. avoidance or social exclusion) are also expressed toward individuals who do not carry pathogens (e.g. physically disabled, disfigured, or obese individuals). In the other words, disgust may act as a signal detection error and operate in a situation where there isn't any real threat or danger.

This theory, as an alternative to the socialization theory of weight bias, considers a pathogen avoidance mechanism as the origin of weight bias. It claims that evolved brain mechanisms allow organisms to detect and avoid infectious stimuli. Similarly, this mechanism may over-generalize to individuals with body types different from the average in the population. Therefore, both obese and skeletally thin frames could act as a sign of infection. This theory also predicts that weight bias is curvilinear; when the target's weight increases or decreases, the perceiver's judgment should become more negative.

Psychological attribution theory

As attribution theory suggests, people search for information about causes of uncertain outcomes. Similarly, after approaching a person with a stigmatized condition like obesity, people search for information about the cause of the condition and then form their reactions to the obese person. In this sense, stigmas could be defined as representations of society's negative perceptions about particular groups. People form their impressions and expectations based on knowledge about society's perceptions around particular groups.

Crandall et al. believe that the obesity stigma is the result of a social ideology; people use negative attributions to explain negative outcomes. Empirical evidence introduces various reasons for obesity including biological, environmental, and/or personal factors. When scholars talk about personal factors, they mean that obese individuals are responsible for being overweight, weight gain or loss is under personal control, and obesity is associated with low self-discipline. If a person believes that obese people are responsible for their fatness, s/he will blame and stigmatize them, whereas individual characteristics outside of personal control such as height or eye color would not be stigmatized. The central notion of this theory is that people get what they deserve in life; they get stigmatized because they deserve it. In this regard, the Protestant work ethic and just world bias are two approaches to explain weight stigma. According to the Protestant work ethic, hard work leads to success. Numerous studies have observed clear patterns between rejection of obese persons and a social ideology of blame. It has been discussed that there is a positive relationship between anti-fat attitudes and variables of political conservatism, symbolic racism, authoritarianism, and the tendency to blame poor individuals. According to the just world bias, the world is a predictable environment in which outcomes depend on a person's effort and ability. This approach leads to a positive bias toward successful people and blame for those who are not. The stereotype of 'beautiful is good' is likely related to just world beliefs. In this stereotype, physically attractive people are attributed more positive qualities than unattractive individuals.

Psychological attribution theory helps to answer questions such as 'why is stigma elicited by obesity, but not thinness?' and 'why is thinness valued?' As an example, people believe that obesity deserves blame while there is no such belief about anorexia. They attribute anorexia and consequently thinness to external factors such as family relationships, mass media, and unrealistic societal ideals of beauty. This predicts that changing attributions of control can lead to reducing negative stigma.

Cultivation theory

Gerbner et al. have introduced television as the primary common source of information and thus socialization. The central claim of their theory, called cultivation, was based on the belief that television programs share similar storytelling features. Cultivation theory examines the long-term effects of television. Gerbner et al. believe that common conceptions of reality are cultivated by the overall pattern of television programs. As the primary proposition of cultivation theory, they state that, compared to light television viewers, heavy television viewers are more likely to believe that social reality aligns with the reality portrayed on television than more objective measures of social reality. Cultivation produces first- and second-order effects. First-order cultivation effects refer to the learning of facts and are related to the relationship between prolonged television exposure and frequency or probability of events or occurrences in social reality. Second-order effects are about people's assumptions about the environment, and assess the relationship between television exposure and general attitudes about the state of the world at large.

Numerous studies have demonstrated that the number of violent acts on U.S. television greatly exceeds the amount of real-world violence in the U.S. Gerbner et al. have also shown that heavy television viewers overestimate the incidence of serious crime in society and are more likely to assess the world as a mean place. They used the term 'mean world syndrome' for this phenomenon; violence-related content of mass media makes viewers believe that the world is where people cannot be trusted and are just looking out for themselves. Although cultivation research first studied television violence, it considered other subjects such as gender roles, political directions, environmental attitudes, science, health, religion, jobs, etc. in following years.

Based on cultivation theory, there may be a positive relationship between childhood television viewing levels and the social reality beliefs in children so that television viewed during childhood may affect the social reality beliefs a person holds as an adult. In the advertising arena, children regularly confront programs and advertising that include overweight characters overeating in a happy context. Repeated exposure to such content can affect children's beliefs about average weight and behavior accepted by the society and lead them to imitate these characters as in-group members.

Social cognitive theory

Social cognitive theory has provided a conceptual framework to examine the mechanisms of the influential role of mass media in society. Based on the social cognitive perspective, human nature is a vast potentiality that can be made into a variety of forms by direct and/or observational experience, depending on biological limits. Social cognitive theory attempts to explain human behavior in terms of a continuous reciprocal interaction between three determinants including personal factors, behavioral patterns, and environmental events (Figure 4.1).

Personal determinants are internal events and include factors such as cognition, self-efficacy, motives, personality, and biological events. Behavioral determinants are aspects of a certain behavior such as complexity, duration, and skill. And finally, environmental events include the context of a social situation, and the roles people hold in that context, models, and relationships.

As discussed earlier, humans have an advanced capacity for observational learning that enables them to expand their knowledge and skills rapidly

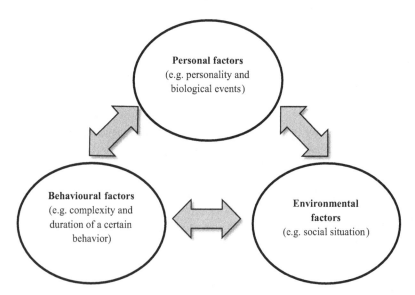

Figure 4.1 Schematization of triadic reciprocal causation in the causal model of social cognitive theory

Source: Adapted from Bandura (2001).

through information conveyed by the rich variety of models. In the other words, cognitive, behavioral, and affective learning can be reached without direct experience, through observing people's actions and the consequences of such actions. Unlike learning by direct experience, observational learning does not require altering the actions of each individual through repeated trial-and-error experiences. Observational learning happens through a single model that can transmit new ways of thinking and behaving simultaneously to numerous people in different places. The modeling aspect of social cognitive theory (or observational learning) occurs based on four conditions: the attention must be directed to the appropriate model, for reasons of attractiveness, competence, status, or similarity, that it is desirable to emulate; remembering what is said or done by the model; converting this information into actions; and finally, being motivated to perform these actions. This theory predicts that children learn from behaviors symbolically modeled in mass media, as well as from real models in their immediate social environment. Most programs and advertising targeting children include characters/models with overweight and or thinness stereotypes. Children usually absorb these characters and likely learn their ways of thinking and behaving through observing these characters' actions and consequences of actions for them.

The effect of overweight stereotypes on children's food choice

A variety of environmental cues influence adults' eating choices that may similarly affect children's choices. Exposure to a stereotype leads to increases in stereotype-consistent behavior, even when the stereotype and/or behavior are negative. For example, exposure to individuals who are overweight can activate the overweight stereotype and lead adults to choose and consume more unhealthy food. Although some research has examined the effect of others' weight on adults' eating choices, there is currently little known about such effects on children.

When children notice the acceptance of stereotypes by others, they develop insights into their social motivations. Awareness of the acceptance of stereotypes by others causes fundamental changes in children's understanding of the social world. According to the perceived social consensus model, stigma and stereotypes are a function of perceptions of other people's stereotypical beliefs. Consensus information may influence the endorsement of racial stereotypes and their subsequent resistance to change. People affiliate and obtain membership, attention, emotional support, acceptance, approval, and security in social groups through sharing information. Individuals will feel more confident in their attitudes when they perceive that other members of the group share their beliefs. Individuals may construct their attitudes based on the perceived attitudes of groups which they consider respectable and/or valued. It means that attitude change would be more likely when information comes from a valued group. Individuals change their endorsement of stereotypes toward different minorities based on positive or negative attitudes held by their valued in-group.

Cartoon characters that are increasingly prevalent in children's and teens' lives (e.g. books, graphic novels, TV shows, movies, video games) have an important influence on activating and accepting some stereotypes in children. Advertisers use cartoon characters or cartoon brand mascots to persuade child audiences. Brand mascots are characteristic figures who can build an identity to help the target market to identify, remember, and understand the brand. These characters can attract children's attention and create positive brand attitudes from early ages. The physical features of these characters may influence child audiences' behaviors, including food behaviors. From early ages, children attribute traits, goals, intentionality, and even human psychology to characters as simplistic as geometric shapes with eyes or faces. Cartoon characters frequently appear to be like humans and children often role-play characters in their games. Given the important role of cartoon characters in children's lives, it is likely that children react to these characters who are similar to humans by applying social stereotypes. Some stereotypes such as sex roles, race, and body weight are formed in children between the ages of 3 and 4. They start to express negative evaluations of body weight around the age of 3. More complex weight stereotypes, similar to those adults use, would appear later, between the ages of 7 and 8. Studies indicate that both positive and negative self-relevant stereotypes are insidious and can affect the performance of even very young children. Unexpectedly, even children as young as 5 years old are susceptible to the activation of identities associated with positive and negative stereotypes. The results of some studies on the effects of stereotypes on children show that child members of a stereotyped group assimilate to the negative aspects of that stereotype when it is made salient. Parasocial relationship theory predicts that familiar characters elicit a positive elaborate affective response, which may subsequently lead children to favor behaviors of and products used by these characters. In other words, children develop parasocial relationships with favorite characters. These emotionally infused relationships or friendships that are made based on characters' attractiveness and the messages they convey can influence children's behaviors, including diet-related ones. So, the effect of depicting overeating as the salient attribute of a cartoon character on children who are not able to distinguish media depictions from reality could be arguable.

Overweight characters can prime children's eating behaviors when two conditions are met. First, the overweight character (cartoon or human) must activate an overweight stereotype. And second, an overweight character increases the accessibility of eating unhealthy foods only if children know about an overweight stereotype, including ideas about eating and/ or unhealthiness. Children usually learn links between eating the wrong foods and being overweight from their parents and schools. As described previously, it is expected that overweight (cartoon) characters on children's programs and advertising prompt children to accept overweight stereotype-consistent behavior and consume more unhealthy food.

Research sample

Title

Children's experience of overweight promotional characters in marketing activities: a phenomenological study.

Objective

Cartoon characters, including promotional characters, are positively associated with children's product recall and attitudes toward advertised products. Because of the increasing prevalence of cartoon characters in children's and teens' lives and their important influence, it is essential to identify the effect of these characters' features on children, not only for commercial companies and marketing practitioners (in order to adhere to their social responsibilities) but also for providers of educational and entertainment programs with a child audience. Accordingly, the aim of this study was to investigate children's experiences of overweight promotional characters and the effect of these characters on their food preferences and behaviors.

Method

In order to deepen understanding of children's experiences, this study used an interpretive approach based on hermeneutic phenomenology research method. Thirteen children, aged 6 to 13 years old, were chosen to participate in this study through the snowball sampling method. To collect data, the method of thematic stories was used. Each participant was asked to tell a story about a picture (Figure 4.2) in 10 minutes that answers some questions (What is it happening? And why? What are characters thinking? What will happen?). Additional questions were asked based on each participant's story and the protocol of study (Figure 4.3) through an in-depth interview. Upon the consent of the participants, the stories were recorded for later transcription. All stages of the study were done considering power

Figure 4.2 Picture of overweight cartoon character

What does this image remind you of?
In your opinion, what is she or he (cartoon character) thinking about?
What has caused this situation?
In your opinion, what are her or his favorite foods?
In your opinion, what kinds of games does she or he like to play?
What do you think of a friend like her or him?

Figure 4.3 Protocol of in-depth interview

imbalance, informed consent, and confidentiality as main considerations of research with children, so that participation was completely voluntary and conducted after consent of the parents; children were assured that all stories and answers were true and interesting for researchers; and they were not pressured into answering questions that they did not want to answer. Data gathering continued until reaching saturation. According to Van Manen's suggestion, data were coded similar to grounded theory approach: open coding was done during reading transcripts; codes were related to each other through the axial coding process, and categories appeared; and finally, themes were extracted through identifying relationships between categories using a selective coding process.

Results

Data were categorized into six themes shown in Table 4.1.

Table 4.1 Themes, categories, descriptions, and interview examples

Themes	Categories	Description	Examples of participants' answers
Attribution of human roles to cartoon characters	Overweight cartoon characters Associated with a friend Associated with a human	Participants gave human roles to cartoon characters, while the human character was usually one of their friends or classmates.	"Reminds me of one of my friends, who eats two big sandwiches every day."
Socialization of physique ideals	Weight stigma Physique ideals The effect of parents	Children evaluate cartoon and human characters they encounter using weight and physique stigmas. In these evaluation processes, participants acted based on physical ideals.	"The teacher said: 'Wow, s/he has lost so much weight. It seems like s/he has done some workout. S/he has eaten less. Let's go and lift her up together.'"
Overweight individuals are responsible The choice theory	Self-deception Overeating Abnormal nutrition Laziness The ability to control obesity	Participants believed that cartoon characters and consequently, overweight individuals, had the ability to control their obesity. In their opinion, overweight individuals resist recommendations provided to them; and they sometimes ignore those recommendations and do the opposite.	"S/he is fat and should go on a diet. S/he must work out using horizontal bar . . . because s/he is not taking care of her-/himself."
Undesirable ending From body to mind	Inefficiency Disease Discrimination	Participants considered both physical and psychological dimensions of the consequences of obesity.	"If s/he is fat, her/his body goes down. My speed increases more. If s/he is chubbier, I can hug or drop her/him."

(Continued)

Table 4.1 (Continued)

Themes	Categories	Description	Examples of participants' answers
Popularity of familiar overweight characters	The need to belong An undesirable playmate Social isolation Weight bias The acceptance of familiar overweight characters	Although participants put great emphasis on the need to belong, they considered the fate of rejection by society for overweight individuals. However, when they talked about a familiar overweight character, things changed.	"I think [Patrick] needs to go on a diet. I feel bad for him. He might get sick later. I wish I could talk to him and give him some advice."
The persuadable role of cartoon characters Desirability and being new as intermediate variables	Persuading the audience to eat Persuading the audience to eat desirable foods Persuading the audience to eat new foods	Participants stated that as they watched cartoon characters like Kung Fu Panda, Patrick, Garfield, and others eat something, they were persuaded to eat as well.	"He [Kung Fu Panda] eats [rice balls] because they are delicious, and he looks cool while eating them."

5 Health messages; as a food product appeal

People have become more health-conscious; they worry about the healthiness of their diet and lifestyle. Such health-related and food-safety issues have reinforced public interest for health information of food products. In response to this trend, food producers added nutrient content and function claims to their marketing activities. Consumers usually make their food decisions based on these health claims and consider the food products healthy if it carries a health claim. But in reality, this health- and nutrition-related information contains some incompatible and contradictory messages regarding risks and benefits.

Health-related claims (such as being low-fat, natural, and providing essential nutrients) or depictions of physical activity (such as gaining strength from product consumption) have become a common phenomenon in food advertising targeting children. Furthermore, in order to convince children, advertisers use items that children have learned at an early age to associate with healthfulness. However, evidence shows that such positive health messages and claims are also appearing on packaging of unhealthful foods.

Nutritional and health marketing

The birth of a new range of food products that are 'better for you' is the result of concerns over health and obesity. Mintel, the global market research firm, observed the rise of new products developed against a backdrop of movement towards healthier and more natural and beneficial foods and beverages for children. This firm reported that a strong and profitable trend has been the claim of 'naturalness' in all cultures; the message that a food or food component is naturally and intrinsically healthy. This trend toward health is now a commonplace.

Food is articulated in the health discourse in television food advertising. As discourse theory discusses, discourse is considered as a partial fixation of meaning, and meaning is achieved through articulation. In simple words, this theory states that the surrounding text of a sentence gives it a deeper meaning. Accordingly, articulation is defined as a practice that establishes a relation among elements (everything outside the discourse) and changes their identity. In food advertising, food can be considered as an element that gains meaning by articulation in the overall health discourse.

Today, foods marketed as natural and healthful are not seen only in the specialty aisles in supermarkets. Rather, natural claims of all types have grown in importance in all regions, and across all categories. However, there is a serious problem in that appeals to health do not necessarily translate into nutritious products. To promote consumption and influence food choice, food marketers may use potentially misleading health claims. Nutritional marketing has appealed to many consumers through the use of nutritional and health claims that draw attention to the nutritional qualities or alleged health benefits of certain products. Evidence shows that this kind of marketing has been able to influence consumers' perceptions about marketed products' nutritional quality and healthiness. Similarly, the results of some experimental studies show that children perceive products with nutrient claims as healthier and tastier, and are more likely to choose energy-dense, nutrient-poor (EDNP) products carrying such claims.

Children prefer products that are fun and made for kid tastes while parents prefer to buy a product that has healthy content for the family. So, food brands trying to reach the child market should appeal to two different groups. Although food brands try to make their food appealing to children by emphasizing the fun aspects, they simultaneously try to make an appeal to parents by emphasizing the fact that their food is good and beneficial for children. A common media used by food producers to broadcast such claims is product packaging, and evidence shows that nearly half of food products have at least one nutrition cue on the package. However, half of these products contain a high amount of saturated fat, sodium, or sugar. Packaging design can also influence consumer perceptions of health through use of color and graphical elements such as pictures or symbols. As discussed, the current trend toward health in packaged food products is set against a backdrop of worldwide policy and regulatory concerns over food marketing to children. In this regard, the World Health Assembly (WHA) has unanimously endorsed recommendations by the WHO to reduce the impact of marketing of foods high in saturated fats, trans-fatty acids, free sugars, and salt on children.

Health message cues such as explicit statements of 'walk regularly' (physical activity message) or 'balance your diet' (healthy diet message) along with an image of a walking person or a healthy dish appear on a large number of televised advertising for unhealthy foods and beverages. Health message claims, such as 'low-fat' or 'zero calories', appearing on food advertising are made to increase the audience's positive attitudes toward the product. Consumers usually infer from nutrition and health claims that the food product is healthy. Such generalizations can result from positivity biases and health halo effects, so that, for example, the mere presence of a low-fat claim may lead to underestimation of calories and greater consumption. In addition, consumers are often confused about low-fat and low-calorie claims. Eating fat-free or low-fat foods does not always lead to weight loss. But consumers will likely make health halo inferences from low-fat and low-calorie claims, which result in a negative relationship between these claims and perceived weight gain risk.

Health halo effect

The health halo effect, as a perceptual error, refers to the act of overestimating the healthfulness of an item based on a single claim. This cognitive bias occurs when an explicit claim about a single health quality or an implicit reference within the marketing (e.g. physical activity depiction) causes more positive impressions about other non-claimed qualities. For example, using the label of 'fruit sugar' instead of 'sugar' can increase the perceived healthiness of a food product. Therefore, a less-healthful food may be considered to be healthy based on the health-related claims. Another relevant example is promoting a candy bar based on having 'half the fat', which causes consumers to experience a halo effect and consider it healthy.

Both explicit and implicit health-related messages work in a similar way in order to manipulate perceptions of food products. The result of an experimental study on these effects is interesting. The study examined the impact of an advertisement for a sugar-laden cereal that depicted physical activity on children's perception, versus an advertisement containing the same product without depicting physical activity. The sugary-cereal advertisement containing physical activity could not encourage children to engage in the depicted physical activity or more general exercise, but it led children to believe that the advertised cereal was a healthier option.

In this regard, two common types of advertising used to market unhealthy foods are nutrient content claims and sports celebrity endorsements. The first, nutrient content claims, highlights positive nutritional attributes of products without mentioning unhealthy nutritional characteristics of the product, and enhances children's perceptions of an unhealthy food product's nutrition content. An example is the claim that a high-sugar cereal is a 'source of fiber'. The second, sports celebrity endorsements, aligns unhealthy products with images of health, vitality, and fame – as an example, McDonald's sponsorship of 2008 Beijing Olympics. In addition, there is some evidence that both nutrient claims and sports celebrity endorsements can increase children's actual food intake.

Theory of priming

The priming theory, derived from the associative network model of human memory, states that media images stimulate related thoughts in the minds of audience members. According to this theory, each idea or concept is stored as a node in a network in relation to other ideas or concepts, connected by semantic paths. The priming occurs when a node in this network becomes activated. This node may act as a filter, an interpretive frame, or a premise for further information processing or judgment formation. Nodes need a threshold for activation and then can stimulate their connected nodes. Each incoming piece of information gets stored in an associative network that contains many pieces of related information. So, people may focus on some aspects of the new information based on their prior networks. Also, cues in the information can trigger one interpretation rather than another.

Similarly, the pairing of positive health messages and unhealthy foods can mislead consumers. Research conducted in this field indicated that people's interpretations of advertised foods depend on their cognitions during the presentation of information; that is, the presentation of a health message may prime consumers to think more positively about their own health than those who did not see a health message. There is some evidence that children also perceive products more positively when the products are presented with a health message. For example, a study found that children prefer the taste of a product if its name references health. It has also been observed that children respond more favorably when a product is promoted as healthful. From the perspective of priming theory, the explanation is that healthful and nutrient content claims emphasize selected nutritional attributes of a product without giving equal prominence to unhealthy nutritional characteristics, which could exaggerate the nutritional quality or health benefit of products.

Format of health messages

Some scholars have stated that the formats of health messages have different impacts on consumer understanding. For example, Scammon found that in television food commercials, only an adjectival format (and no numerical format) can influence consumers' perceptions and product choices. She also found that consumers could not control the amount of time the disclosures appeared on the screen and thus the more complex numerical disclosures are difficult for them to process. Consumers' perceptions of products' nutritional quality are influenced by exposure to print advertising with simplified nutrition information, and advertising containing more complex nutrition information disclosures do not affect consumers' perceptions. This evidence shows that in addition to the provision of nutrition information, the format of presenting such information can influence consumers' choices too.

Studies and regulatory requirements have almost exclusively focused on the verbal content and wording of health messages and ignored the structural issues, such as executional elements in food advertising. In this sense, more focus is needed on audiovisual processing of televised messages and fine-print disclosures. The results of comparing print-plus-audio to single presentations have indicated that the effect of print-plus-audio is superior to audio alone. Moreover, materials containing pictures and audio have been recognized as more effective than materials involving audio and printed (words) by some studies. These studies claim that combining pictures with print or audio generally maximizes learning. Finally, other research has documented that audiovisual cues can be more meaningful than a single modality because of their synergetic effects. Meanwhile, in criticism of the fine-print disclosure practice in television advertising, critics argue that viewers are unlikely to be able to read the messages because of the small print size and the brevity of their appearance. In addition, using fine-print disclosures in television commercials can be effective if messages appear at the beginning and end of advertising – the primacy and recency effects.

Health knowledge

Having knowledge about a topic affects an individual's ability to process and elaborate on topic-relevant arguments in advertising. Since consumer nutrition knowledge is generally poor, effects of knowledge on weight management are not strong enough. As Brucks et al. found, although consumers use nutritional information in early stages of information processing such as the attention stage, they do not tend to engage more in the subsequent processing stages. Recent research also suggests that a general level of health and nutrition knowledge often has little impact on consumer food choices.

Health is defined as mental, physical, and social aspects of well-being, and health knowledge is related to the health consequences of the behaviors. Children have diverse ways to interpret various forms and content of information aimed at improving their health and this is considered a complex problem in health promotion activities targeting children. Knowledge acquisition is a central concept in health promotion for children; they need health promotion programs and campaigns in which they can actively participate. In this regard, Brinkmann, based on identity theory, presented his interesting approach by focusing on individuals' self-interpretation (or social imaginary), that is, the ways people imagine their social existence. It is the set of values, institutions, laws, and symbols common to a particular social group that determines how group members fit together, how things go on between them and others, the expectations that are normally met, and the deeper normative images that underlie these expectations. This approach can describe how children acquire health knowledge and act accordingly. This process is based on children's imagination of healthy or unhealthy behavior in order to fit together, and their interconnected identity structures. Health knowledge acquisition is a constant process of observation and recognition, and the different knowledge structures create different conditions for relating knowledge to interpretations of identity.

Motivation and understanding are two essential criteria for effective healthy eating promotion. Often, children do not feel the urgency associated with health issues. They generally conceptualize healthy food as adult food, boring, dull, tasteless, expensive, and inaccessible. For children, healthy foods are associated with homemade foods, weight loss, and being at home. In contrast, they associate fast food or junk food with pleasure, friends, and independence. So, motivation to eat a healthy diet is known to be a problem among children.

There is some evidence that even quite young children associate thinness with health. Most of them feel too fat and express guilt about eating. They are aware that they need food for growth, health, or energy, and that vitamins and fiber are good for them while sugar and fat are bad for them. Despite children's understanding of basic nutrition facts, they do not tend to select foods in alignment with this knowledge. Some studies have showed that the healthiness of the food is not a very important factor in children's food choice. Rather, they usually choose food based on their personal preferences for the taste, texture, and appearance of the food. However, many nutritionists are not concerned about the difference in nutritional value between the healthy choices and the favorite choices. They argue that meals chosen based on preference are, in many respects, no less healthy than food chosen based on children's perceptions of the healthiness of the meal, and sometimes the preferred meals are even healthier.

According to cognitive development theory, children in the preoperational stage are very focused on perceptual properties of stimuli and have the tendency to concentrate on a single dimension of evaluating an object. As children grow up, they can consider other dimensions of a stimulus (such as healthiness) at the same time and compare them. This theory can justify the efforts to teach health knowledge to children, because there is the hope that children will finally be able to use such knowledge to make their own choices and behaviors. According to the associative network model of human memory, when a cue activates children's stored knowledge, they will be able to use this knowledge to control their responses. Health messages placed in food advertising can work as cues to activate children's health knowledge.

However, excess effort to teach children about food could reverse the targeted effect. This is usually explained with commodity theory, which has been built on the assumption that any goods that are seemingly unavailable are consequently deemed as more desirable. Accordingly, after heavily education about food and food intake, children may show the reverse behavior and choose food low in nutritional value.

Counter-advertising

Counter-advertising is defined as advertising that responds to or disproves the claims of other advertising. Therefore, advertising is not only used to tout a product or service, but it can also take a stand against other advertisements in regard to controversial topics.

Counter-advertising could reduce the persuasive effects of promotions on children. However, as children's cognitive abilities are not fully developed (see the cognitive development theory discussion), it is not yet clear how counter-advertising works to make children more resistant to commercial food promotions. Petty and Priester's elaboration likelihood model (ELM) can be used to explain potential effects of counter-advertising on children's behavior. Along with food product advertising, variables such as characteristics of the communication's source, message, and/or receiver can influence (or moderate) the persuasive potential effect of food promotion counter-advertising. Counter-advertising may persuade children to change their attitudes and behavior toward unhealthy food advertising through the central or peripheral routes. The central route is taken when children's involvement with food choice is high and thus they process information more actively. In contrast, the peripheral route is taken when there is not enough motivation to think about the argument and children prefer to use simple persuasive cues without active information processing to react to the advertising. As discussed in Chapter 3, food marketers commonly prefer using peripheral cues such as sports celebrity endorsements. However, for counter-advertising, both potential routes should be used for persuasion. Practitioners employ peripheral factors to engage children who are not motivated to attend to these messages, and employ central factors under the conditions of high involvement with food choice and health outcomes via integrating strong logical information into children's belief structure.

Counter-advertising usually draws children's attention to negative health effects of certain products, questions the motives of producers or advertisers of certain products, or reveals misleading promotions. Nutrient content claims and sports celebrity endorsements of unhealthy foods, as two common types of unhealthy food marketing, are countered by advertising portraying the unhealthy components of these foods and the unpleasant consequences of regularly consuming them. Counter-advertising also uses peripheral cues such as expert support for reputable health organizations and/or child-oriented designs to capture children's attention. Promoting this specific form of advertising literacy could empower children to identify, analyze, and critically evaluate commercial messages. According to Harris et al.'s food marketing defense model, in order to withstand the persuasive appeal of advertising, people need to be aware that they are being targeted. They also need to understand how exposure to advertising can affect them. As children's media literacy levels increase with age, the probability of being persuaded by high-quality arguments (taking the central route) increases. But younger children likely prefer peripheral advertising cues.

Regulations

To gather information about foods, consumers use a wide variety of sources, such as a health standpoint, the information on the food product label, and food advertising. Nutrition labels and health claims are two types of information appearing on food products. These days, all packaged foods have labels that provide essential nutrient and ingredient information. This is a result of the Nutrition Labeling and Education Act (NLEA) passed by the U.S. Congress in 1990 and enacted in 1994. This act requires all food producers to present standardized nutrition facts (such as highlighting the percentages of fat and cholesterol, serving size, and percentage of daily value) on the package. The aim of NLEA was to help consumers choose more healthful foods and thereby promote better health outcomes.

Health claims in advertising have transformed markets from purely focused on matters of taste, convenience, and other factors unrelated to health into markets in which promotion focuses on health. Considering a place for health-related status of food product in food advertising could improve public health by assisting consumers in making better-informed food choices. Specific mention of nutrient content in food advertising can have a positive impact on people's dietary habits, if such information goes beyond exaggerated, unrealistic claims. As the Federal Trade Commission (FTC) expressed, there is the concern that consumers draw misleading conclusions from such claims. Therefore, some type of disclosure is needed about the related negative nutrient, such as fat, saturated fat, cholesterol, or sodium. From a regulatory perspective, the nutritional profile of unhealthy foods with health claims has always been a controversial issue.

According to a WHO study on global advertising regulations on health claims, regulations have focused on one of two forms: the extension of the regulations on the use of health claims in labeling to the use of claims in advertising, and insertion of the clauses related to the use of health claims in advertising consistent with regulations on advertising and/or health. However, due to the unique nature of message processing in advertising, the health claims placed in advertising should be regulated differently from those for product labels and packages.

Research sample

Title

Effects of nutrient content claims, sports celebrity endorsements, and premium offers on pre-adolescent children's food preferences: experimental research.

Objective

Nutrient content claims tend to focus on some nutritional attributes of a product without giving equal information about unhealthy nutritional characteristics. Such claims could exaggerate the nutritional quality or health benefit of products. As some studies revealed, children usually perceive products with a nutrient content claim as healthier. The aim of this study was to assess the effect of nutrient content claims and two other types of food promotion (sports celebrity endorsements and premium offers) on children's perceptions of child-oriented food products, compared to a control condition with no on-pack promotions.

Method

A between-subjects experimental design was conducted with the purpose of testing children's responses to three common food marketing techniques. To accomplish this aim, front-of-pack promotions for EDNP (energy-dense and nutrient-poor) food products were varied to represent four conditions: no promotion (control), nutrient content claims, sports celebrity endorsement, and premium offer. Five food product categories (including sweetened breakfast cereal, cheese dip snacks (savory), ice cream bars (sweet), frozen chicken nuggets (quick meal), and flavored milk drinks) were chosen to test packaging effects within each condition. For each of the five product categories, packs were prepared based on four experimental conditions. Children completed measures after choosing their preferred product. In the nutrient content claim condition, two positive nutritional attributes of the product were highlighted. For the condition of sports celebrity endorsement, an image of a popular Australian male athlete and an associated competition were featured. And for the condition of premium offer, a free prize upon purchasing the product was offered.

To redirect participants' attention to something other than the experimental manipulation, they were informed that during the survey they would be asked about their views on some food products. To measure children's product preference, they were presented with their assigned EDNP food pack and healthier comparison pack side-by-side on screen and asked, 'If you had the choice of these two products, which one would you want more?' To measure children's perception of food products' nutrients, questions were asked on a 7-point Likert scale. For a manipulation check, paired sample t-tests were conducted. Participating in the study were 1,302 children (grade 5 and 6 students). They were selected from government primary schools in metropolitan Melbourne, Australia. To analyze the data, logistic regression analysis (to test differences between promotion conditions on participants' preference for the EDNP product in the choice task) and analysis of variance (ANOVA) tests (to test for mean differences in ratings of the EDNP product packs by promotion condition) were conducted. To observe the principles of studies involving children, the Human Research Ethics Committee of Cancer Council Victoria, the Department of Education and Early Childhood Development Victoria, and principals of participating schools approved the study. Moreover, participants returned the consent forms signed by their parents or carers.

Results

Results of this study showed a significant effect of front-of-pack promotions on children's preference and perceptions of the ENDP product. Nutrient content claims made children more likely to choose EDNP products and increased their perceptions of these products' nutrient content compared to the control condition. Sports celebrity endorsements made boys more likely to choose EDNP products but this technique did not influence girls' product preferences. Premium offers had little effect on children. Overall, trends showed that nutrient content claims and sports celebrity endorsements enhanced participants' perceptions of EDNP products' healthiness and the health of consumers of this product. Although nutrient content claims are usually considered adult-targeted informational appeals, this study showed that these promotions also persuade children (Dixon et al., 2013).

6 Food product placement
Integration of advertising and entertainment

Product placement or brand placement is defined as the location or the integration of a product or a brand into the entertainment world. Seeing brands everywhere is annoying for some individuals, while some people may derive amusement from seeing and identifying brands. Product placement has increasingly become a part of our daily lives; in spite of that, people love it or hate it. In such a world, brands are able to get closer to their target audience through films, television programs or series, plays, novels, songs, shows, and even video games. This current trend uses communication lines different from the three main types (above the line, below the line, and internet marketing). Entertainment marketing is the term that is sometimes used to describe the experiential consumption deriving from brand and product placements.

Product placement is a marketing strategy that places products in a visible context different from a typical marketing context. Although products sometimes are visible in television shows or movies, products are not often the focus on these programs, and the products do not fit into the context of the programs. Product integration, as a special type of product placement, is placing an advertised product as a central point of the programs' content. Product placement is also used by media production agents in order to provide realism to movie and television scenes, and to influence viewers through increased brand awareness and product endorsement. Product placement is a marketing strategy usable for different media such as network and cable television, films, radio, music, videos and DVDs, books, plays, video games, and advergames. It is an important strategy to reach people who have grown up and lived using technology and turn to new media for entertainment and information.

Meanwhile, contemporary children's media culture has also changed. Children spend more time using a variety of electronic media, especially the internet and electronic game playing. However, the percentage of marketing budgets spent on television advertising has declined in recent years, and marketers have increased their use of interactive marketing techniques such as video games and viral and buzz marketing. Therefore, responsible food marketing to children tends to use new media (e.g. advergames) to reach young consumers, although older media such as television and packaging remain equally important.

Reasons for product placement

Today, consumers need to use strategies to protect their psychic liberty more than ever. They usually look for ways to avoid the clutter in our current commercialized world such as the presence of a greater number of companies, less product differentiation, adoption of shorter advertising formats, and an increase in the amount of commercial time. In order to exist, a brand must be known, at least by those who are likely to buy its products. So, it must connect with this potential audience. Marketing and entertainment have always been allies. From the beginnings of radio until today, many programs have been produced or simply financed by major brands. In a time period, for example, the cinema turned into a fad and reached the height of its popularity. And consequently, it was quickly perceived as a vector of huge potential. Cinema, as a captive medium, has been interesting to advertisers.

There are hundreds of radio stations and television channels, thousands of daily newspaper and magazine media, tens of millions of internet sites – so much that an entire lifetime on this earth would not be long enough to visit them all. There are also new books, new songs, new shows, and new movies that arrive each day to enlarge the communications environment. Nonetheless, there are still only 24 hours in a day and 7 days in a week. This situation has become worse with the increasing sales of pre-recorded programs, via download or video on demand. These programs are going to obtain more and more share of the small screen. Studies show that people spend more time on the internet than in front of the television set. As the computer screen superseded the home television set, advertisers faced a new problem: when consumers are playing on their consoles, they cannot be exposed to television advertising. Such a state of affairs led to a profound change in the communications environment. With this change, brand managers would make more effort to retain the attention of a few consumers by placing the brand in a good position.

Benefits of product placement

Product and brand placement have created numerous advantages for advertisers, particularly when they have few resources in comparison to their competitors. Product placement is not a communication technique reserved only for the world's leading brands. Other groups such as smaller actors and challengers can also use it. It is important to know that consumers do not like distracting placements. In the other words, the nature of the placement should first be consistent with the advertiser's objectives. Next, it also depends on the imperatives of the production and the director's wishes.

There is evidence that the viewers' anti-advertising defenses are lowered at the cinema and thus, brand awareness can be concretely reinforced. The brands that are more seen or heard have more chance to be remembered, so the consumer may conclude that such brands are very well known. Of course, not all product placements share the same fate. The vast majority of studies conducted on product placement show an overall tolerance among audiences for the placement of products or brands. In order to benefit from a positive perception, a rule should be respected in product placement: the rule of a tolerable and justified presence. It means a natural logic between the product and the nature of the program. A well-organized product or brand placement is positive not only for brand awareness, but also for the brand's image. It is important that product placement is not about sales; rather, it is about brand awareness. However, the advertisers of the twenty-first century are not confident about the effectiveness of this strategy. Although numerous studies have verified the impact of placement on sales, there are a large number of uncontrollable exogenous variables.

Types of branded entertainment

Series and television programs

Television series are a favorite media for advertisers. Their large audiences, fewer commercial breaks, and short format suitable for the seduction of modern consumers are some reasons for their popularity with advertisers. Some series can maintain a high quality because of their fairly large production budgets, comparable to movie budgets, so they are likely to retain their audience from episode to episode over several seasons. Using recurring characters as a distinctive feature of a series is also a certain advantage for product and brand placements. Despite these facts, placement in a television series is not without risks. Due to intensifying competition, television channels are now particularly quick to shift a series to another time slot, or even to cancel it if it does not gain an audience as expected. Also, television reality shows are also serious competitors with a considerable target audience and the flexibility of brand integration that is possible.

Product placement is prohibited by law in programs directed at children, but it is common in prime-time television programs. The majority of brand appearances usually occur in prime-time programs. Product placements are also abundant in children's and teens' movies. In the 2002 movie *Spider-Man*, the action hero used his web-spinning capabilities to retrieve a can of Dr Pepper to quench his thirst. Heinz ketchup was featured in the movie *Scooby Doo*. A character in *Spy Kids 2* opened a lunch box including items such as a Big Mac, French fries, and a carbonated soft drink with the golden arches of the McDonald's Corporation. In an experimental study, children were shown amended versions of a brief movie clip from a popular movie. Half of children watched the clip including a prominent branded carbonated soft drink and the other half watched the clip without the branded carbonated soft drink. Children who were exposed to the branded clip selected the branded soft drink more frequently after the viewing.

Novels

Brands and/or products are placed in a novel in order to add description and aid development of a mental image to support the story. Because of the evocative power of brands, the author may place brand(s) in the novel to power the reader's imagination. Therefore, even best-selling authors use brand placement. Of course, the financial aspect of such placements is a strong motive.

Song lyrics

In today's modern and commercial world, brands are even present in song lyrics. This approach is called brand dropping. The integration of branded beverage products into popular songs is a new type of product placement. Researchers argue that listeners usually orient their behavior in the direction of the lyrics through the simple schematic process. Moreover, the variation of musical genres in our current age is another advantage for songs to be considered as a medium to reach a specific target audience. Certain musical niches can be used to reach certain population segments, especially the youth segment that is usually pessimistic about the content of traditional advertising messages. Rappers also provoke such pessimism by criticizing television in the lyrics of their songs. Like novels, some media and entertainment companies actively seek brand-spot placements of their products to make their art more real. On the other hand, there is a big demand by industries for placement of their brands in song lyrics and music videos.

Branded video games and advergames

In the 1980s, advertising banners first appeared in arcade racing games. Financial support was the primary motivation of game developers to insert a brand into a video game. The production costs of video games are rising sharply, and successful titles that exceed the profitability threshold are rare. For advertisers, this market is highly concentrated so that only three console manufacturers – Sony, Microsoft, and Nintendo – control almost the entire market.

In comparison with a movie, placement in a video game has additional advantages for advertisers: the player generally pays much closer attention than the movie viewer; there is greater possibility to control and overcome the environment for players; and there are also possibilities for verification before mass production of the game that is derived from the flexibility of insertion methods in a wholly created graphic universe, compared with the movies. The virtual universe of the game has become increasingly realistic. Instead of anonymous characters, sports games benefit from the indirect effect of famous sportspersons through avatars that are alter egos of the real professionals. It is clear that such realistic games need real brands. In other words, if a game is set in the real world but ignores brands or inserts fictional logos, this could actually damage the game by distancing it from the reality of the universe. According to research evidence, players have a positive attitude toward placements in more realistic games. Although video game developers previously paid companies for use of their logos and/or brands in video games, now the situation has changed and brand placement is a source of revenue for video game manufacturers.

Modern children spend a lot of time using a variety of electronic media, especially the internet and electronic game playing. Advertising clutter, as a common phenomenon in recent years, has had some consequences, including less advertising viewing, more advertising avoidance, lower advertising memory, reducing the audience's ability to properly recognize the brand, and an undesirable impact on customers' emotional responses to advertising. Because of these negative effects of advertising clutter, advertisers are looking for new and nontraditional ways to engage customers. They have increased the proportion of marketing budgets spent on interactive marketing techniques such as video games and viral and buzz marketing. Online tools are popular tactics for reaching children. Advergames are a powerful online tool that deliver messages interactively and make the player engage in ways that traditional one-way media, such as television, cannot. Children often cannot recognize the advertising intent of advergames, as these games blur the line between entertainment content and persuasive messages. According to persuasion knowledge model (PKM), over time consumers develop personal knowledge about the tactics used in marketers' persuasion attempts. This knowledge helps them identify how, when, and why marketers try to influence them. Accordingly, they select coping tactics believed to be effective and appropriate. But children have not developed persuasion knowledge and often cannot differentiate advertising from entertainment content. Therefore, they do not usually understand the persuasive intents of the advertisers. Even for older children who have obtained more developed persuasion knowledge, the context of an advertising exposure can distract them and make it more difficult for them to defend against advertising. The interactive and engaging gaming experience do not let persuasion knowledge become activated. Therefore, advergames can have a stronger effect on children's brand awareness, preferences for the food brands, and food consumption behaviors than TV or print advertising. Moreover, according to the cue reactivity theory, food cues in advergames signal food intake, which subsequently acts as conditioned stimuli that triggers conditioned responses, such as cravings and actual eating behavior. The use of language in advergames is usually limited to brand names display. It is argued that interactive and brand-centered advergames provide immersive opportunities to strengthen brand images.

On the other hand, due to their graphic and interactive nature, advergames can cause false memory. Advergames request active attention and participation of players, and playing the game is the major activity for a game player that grabs their primary attention. The food cues that are highly embedded in the content of the game are not the central object of attention. Therefore, advertisers want to know whether their brand names/logos are actually being observed by the gamers or not. As the limited capacity model of attention assumes, people need mental resources for processing messages, and at any given point of time, they have a limited sum of mental resources. When the resources allocated to the subprocesses of information processing (i.e. encoding, storage, and retrieval) are not sufficient, the receiver's memory suffers for that particular message. For example, cognitive overload may limit the encoding of a specific message and result in poor recognition levels. According to this model, multitasking divides an individual's total mental capacity into two parts: capacity for the primary task and capacity for the secondary task. As was discussed previously, playing the game is the primary task for the game players and processing the brand or product placements is the secondary task. Therefore, fewer mental resources will remain for processing in-game placements.

To conclude, the most effective advergames are product-relevant games, which are accomplished by building games that engage players in activities related to a behavior they would do if they purchased the placed brand's product. This enhances implicit associations between game content and behaviors.

Entertainment experience of advertising and children's food choice

As discussed earlier, companies have started engaging customers in new and nontraditional ways by using online media. Placement of the company's products/brands in online media is one such new technique. Some advantages over traditional advertising media include high involvement with the brand, effectively conveying subtle associations, familiarity, and having a fun experience. Placement of advertising in the background of the games also gives a feeling of realism to the customers and increases product likeability once a child is attracted by the fun dimension of a product. Games, movies, and television shows offer favorable contexts for effective transfer of affect because the brands placed in them are completely integrated into an entertainment experience. Product preferences are enhanced by placements in movies and games.

According to cognitive and social development approaches, play is the primary activity by which children assign meaning to things. Accordingly, children use play as a resource to give sense to the commercial world they are immersed in. Advergames could be more persuasive to customers than traditional advertising and might appeal to children. It is estimated that on average, the amount of time spent on an advergame is about 7 to 30 minutes, which is significantly higher than the time spent on a television advertisement.

Exposure to food commercial messages and media content at the same time can blur boundaries between advertising, entertainment, and information. Because they evoke a certain degree of activity, advergames engage players with interactive content rather than just passively exposing them to it. Entertainment plays an important role in the persuasion process and entertained children are more likely to evaluate the embedded food product/brand more positively. Furthermore, the complete integration of a food brand into the entertainment experience facilitates the transfer of positive affect from the medium to the food through classical conditioning.

More recent studies confirm that children choose snacks that were being advertised on advergames significantly more compared with others that were not advertised. The American Academy of Pediatrics has made the statement that interactive online marketing of calorie-dense, low-nutrient foods may be contributing to childhood obesity. Indeed, evidence supports the potentially powerful impact of advergames on persuading children to prefer, choose, and request food categories and brands.

Research sample

Title

The role of advertising on children's food choice: a mixed method research.

Objective

Overweight children are more likely to become overweight adults. Along with parents and schools' effects, advertising contributes to children's consumption patterns. Despite researchers' focus on TV advertising targeting children, children today spend more time using a variety of electronic media, especially the internet and electronic games. Digitalization has changed children's media environment over the past decade. The advergame is a new marketing technique derived from this change that has provided a more entertaining brand/product experience than traditional media forms. Accordingly, this study aimed at a better understanding of children's food choice in the real world conditions in which children are exposed to different advertising (with different levels of entertainment) containing food and characters simultaneously.

Method

A 2 (Food type: healthy vs. unhealthy) × 2 (Body build prime: normal vs. overweight cartoon character) × 2 (Entertainment experience: low vs. high) full-factorial, randomized, between-subject experimental design was utilized. To accomplish the aim of the study, variables of food type and body build prime were placed in versions of (visual) advertising and advergames. Four versions of the same advertising were designed: with an overweight cartoon character (adopted from initial qualitative research (see Chapter 4)) eating unhealthy food; with an overweight cartoon character eating healthy food; with a normal weight cartoon character eating unhealthy food; and with a normal weight cartoon character eating healthy food. Four versions of the game were also designed using the same combinations of advertising, but with consideration of the games' attributes. Each participant was randomly assigned to different versions of advertising or the game in the schools' chapel.

To measure children's food choice, the children were asked to choose between several alternate foods (12 snacks based on Iranian culture and eating habits depicted on two cards with six snacks on each). Pictorial cues were used in the questionnaires because they were easy for children to understand, organize, and communicate their choices in an enjoyable and playful way. After assigning children to one of the eight experimental conditions, they were asked to imagine that their parents went to work and that they asked the researcher to take care of him or her while they were out (in order to prevent experimenter expectancy). But the researcher does not know her or his favorite foods. So, she or he could help the researcher by checking three out of six snack items on each card that was shown to him or her. Answers were entered on a 7-point scale into SPSS. To evaluate the credibility and general understanding of the advertising, the game (manipulation check), and the questionnaire, two pretests were conducted with 10 children.

A total of 12 elementary schools (497 children) aged 6 to 11 years old participated in the experiment. To analyze the data, general linear models with food choice as the dependent variable were used. To observe the principles of studies involving children, the ethical principles according to the British Psychological Society (including respect, competence, responsibility, and integrity) and the American Psychological Association (APA) (such as institutional approval, informed consent to research, and informed consent for recording voices and images in research) were respected.

Results

The results of this study supported the effect of entertainment level, as a moderating variable, on children's food choice. The results showed that exposure to unhealthy food items (vs. healthy items) and overweight cartoon characters (vs. normal weight) led children to choose more unhealthy foods. But these effects were more pronounced in the condition of more entertaining advertising (advergame vs. TV advertising). These results were consistent with the literature that claims the use of fun increases children's recall, food preferences, purchase requests, and consumption behavior. Therefore, with the greater effect of a higher level of entertainment on children's behavior taken into account (and noting that some of games transfer real life activities to the virtual world), much care should be taken in choosing the characters of these games and the products that they consume (Esmaeilpour, Heidarzadeh, Mansourian, & Khounsiavash, 2017b).

7 Marketing research and children

Childhood studies are related to the ways in which childhood is represented or socially constructed. Representations of childhood are common in a range of fields and materials including history, autobiography, sociology, psychology, children's books, studies of educational practice, and media analysis. The multi-disciplinary and eclectic attribution of childhood studies is both its strength and weakness. Its strength is due to its ability to make fascinating and unexpected connections between disparate fields (like autobiography and social history, studies of play and children's fantasy, cognitive psychology and book illustration, book illustration and children's art, quality fiction and television soaps, computer games and moral development). On the other hand, this attribution may cause a struggle to convince practitioners of these disciplines that the insights of research can be reached in any other way than by being eclectic.

Granville Stanley Hall is known as the father of childhood-related subjects. Despite changing their approach to the nature of childhood across decades, Hall et al.'s major achievement was highlighting the importance of the childhood period and its impact on social affairs. Another part of the efforts in this field was publishing dozens of specialized journals such as *European Early Childhood Education Research Journal* and *International Journal of Child-Computer Interaction* in recent decades. Accordingly, a broad range of studies are related to the concept of 'childhood'. Although each field has its particular perspective, sense-making of childhood is their common point.

Perspectives of childhood

Yet, the term 'childhood' begs many questions: 'when does childhood begin?', 'does childhood change with time?', 'is and was childhood different for boys and for girls?', 'is childhood different in different countries or towns?', 'is childhood different in working-class or middle-class families?', 'are children miniature versions of adults or are they something separate?', etc.

In order to define childhood, it is logical to look at ways in which people have tried to define childhood over the years. Some definitions emphasized the innocence of children, being close to God and the angels, not yet contaminated by the evil and cynicism of adults; something like Locke's concept of the 'tabula rasa'. Rousseau's natural child is a version of this innocence. Another definition that relied on similar assumptions stressed the innate wickedness of children; deliberate, weak wickedness that is not yet versed in the ways of prayer and self-improvement. According to this approach, the purpose of prayer and education was to put this wickedness right and improve children. This was a view held by Hannah More, author of *Strictures on the Modern System of Female Education*.

In addition to ideas of children as good or bad, and of childhood as a period of innocence or evil, there was the idea of child as a force for good, who brought deathbed penitence among villains. Based on this idea, children's power for good often survived in wretched and corrupting environments (as numerous Evangelical novels in the nineteenth century, such as *Oliver Twist*, show) despite being surrounded by evil. In this regard, Postman argued that this kind of innocence was threatened by the postmodernism of modern culture and media that broke down the secret complexity of the adult world for children, and so caused the disappearance of childhood. Of course, this interpretation of childhood creates questions about innate innocence and protectability, and is an argument rehearsed in the discussion of censorship or the effects of advertising.

Another perspective emphasized children's rights as full social beings and not as miniature versions of adults or symbols of goodness. According to this approach, children are different from adults, develop and sustain their own culture, and have their own rules. This approach considers childhood as a much more complex issue than merely something dependent on the state of adulthood. It is looking to answer questions of 'what do adults mean when they talk about protecting children's rights and providing for their needs, bringing them up, punishing them, indicating boundaries, and helping them deal with their fears?' Opies helped to identify this independent area of childhood through highlighting the quality of their own culture in many of their games, rhymes, and interactions. These ideas are used in studies on bullying, domestic violence, and consumerist harassment.

These perspectives on childhood show that the area of childhood studies is rich and it is important to study the historical and social context of childhood. Overall, researchers should consider all important historical, theological, and ideological perspectives on childhood before beginning their studies on childhood and its social and cultural context.

Developing child-centric research

During last 30 years, different methodologies and techniques have been used in research with children. Traditional positivistic methodologies used in research with children have emphasized large-scale quantitative observation, measurement, and assessment of children and viewed children as mere objects to be studied. This group of methodologies carried out research on, rather than with, children. Moreover, such research has been formed based on adult assumptions and focused on adult interests rather than the interests of children.

In the 1990s, new ways of working with children repositioned children's voices at the center of the research process and were fair and respectful to children as subjects, rather than objects, of the research. It is clear that researchers are adults with more experience, physical presence, institutional positioning, and social standing and have greater status over their child participants. Therefore, researchers have begun to search for ways to combat these unequal power relations in the pursuit of more child-friendly research. As a key way of addressing this issue of power relations, child-centric research methods were suggested that were based on children's preferred methods of communication. For many children, traditional methods such as questionnaire surveys are inappropriate or boring. New methodologies of representation enable children to communicate through drawing, photography, stories or songs, etc. that are attractive for children. In such techniques, age is not synonymous with children's abilities. The aim is to build rapport, trust, and confidence with participants. Researchers must evaluate their research in terms of the degree of achieving meaningful participation, rather than adopt a tokenistic view and make some symbolic efforts.

Child-centric research methods

Children's photographs

Although photographs are not unbiased documentaries of the social and material world, they are at least good tools to anticipate the characteristic attributes of photographer. They have many things to tell about their photographer, the technology used to produce the photographs, and the events or things they depicted. They can also help discover and demonstrate the relationships that may be overlooked. Photography gives an active role to children in data gathering and can build a bridge between the child participants and researchers. This is an increasingly popular child-centric research method.

Children can easily use disposable or instant cameras, and then explore and record their own experiences, feelings, and sense of place(s) – their own practical observations of their experiences. This is a beneficial method, particularly for working with children with poor written or verbal literacy. Giving the responsibility of a camera to children can lead to build a trustful relationship with the researcher. Since this method does not require the presence of researchers in the time of photograph taking, this avoids the researcher's interference in the dynamics of the space being captured. The method of photography also empowers children because children do not have spatial and temporal restrictions on their participation in the project. However, using photography as a child-centric research method may cause some critical issues around the interpretation, meaning, and representation of pictures. Researchers should ascertain children's own reasons for taking photographs, rather than giving their own interpretation and assumptions to the pictures.

Projective technique

This method engages children in task-centered activities that exploit their particular talents and interests. Therefore it can provide a good way of allowing children to express their ideas and opinions, rather than the use of more talk-centered methods such as interviews and questionnaires. Although these activities are not fun for all children, drawing usually enables children to express themselves and communicate freely. Like photography, drawing is an appropriate method for children with low literacy skills, and is a process in which children are in control and researchers do not need to be present. Again, similar to using photographs, it is necessary to have children's participation in interpretation of the drawing to ensure that the drawing represents the child's meaning, rather than that of the researchers.

Diaries

The diary is a personal account of one's life. It can provide a sense of intimacy and allow children to freely record feelings and experiences that are embarrassing or challenging for them to discuss in an interview setting. One of the methodological issues of using diaries as a research technique is that asking children to express their own views and concerns does not always result in the production of information directly relevant to the research. In other words, children's responses may not explicitly reveal direct answers to research questions. Their answers may highlight issues and experiences important to their own lives that can provide insights into daily routines and interactions with family members.

Questionnaires

Questionnaire surveys are not known as child-friendly methods. Moreover, the usefulness and applicability of quantitative methods in child-centered research are doubtful. Large-scale, quantitative data collection is needed to situate children's lives within the wider socio-politico-economic context. There are also debates around the practical design of questionnaire surveys to create a more child-friendly method. In this regard some innovative techniques, such as pictorial Likert scales and the use of open questions, allow children some freedom to structure their responses. Yet, quantitative data can be usable in providing information for implementation of children's rights and also in providing international comparisons about children's economic position.

Electronic measurement

Along with technological advances, a number of new electronic devices for marketing and media research have emerged. New electronics are an appealing way for children to participate in research. Some useful electronic tools are detailed as follows:

> *Arbitron's Personal People Meter* (PPM), also known as Nielsen Meter, is a small device the size of a pager that picks up audio signals from any medium or venue that is encoded. It has been used to measure how many people are exposed or listening to individual radio stations and television stations, including cable television. Its benefit for children's measurement is that participation is passive. Children are not required to write anything down, push any buttons, or attempt to identify the media entities they hear.
>
> *MindSet*, a MindShare tool, measures real-time responses to over 60 different types of communication channels. It works by a personal digital assistant (PDA) device that asks participants to respond to some questions, including their location and channels they notice. This technique can be used for older children.
>
> *Online studies* work well with children. Children have grown up in an online environment and actively enjoy going online. In addition, the anonymity derived from the web allows them to be more honest.

Children as researchers

Involvement of children in the research process can help with understanding the structural, situational, and personal complexity of their lives. Todays, researchers acknowledge the value of children's interpretations and accounts. Children are not only research respondents; they are also involved in different stages of the research process, including setting the agenda, choosing topics of investigation, collecting information, interpreting and disseminating findings, and acting upon them. After the 1989 Convention on the Rights of the Child, there has been increased awareness of the value of child participation in different scopes, including in research. Consequently, increasing interest has been created in the methodological aspects of conducting research with children, including informed consent and confidentiality, the role of gatekeepers, the use of child-centric techniques, children's understanding of their research rights, children's perspectives on the methods used in research, issues of power and representation, ethics of research, and participatory methodologies.

Christensen and James identified four ways to view children and childhood in research, including children as objects, children as subjects, children as social actors, and children as co-researchers. The perspective of children as co-researchers recognizes children as capable and competent agents who are able to build the aspects of their culture and social world through different forms of interaction. Therefore, children are experts in their own lives because they are able to construct their own social situations. Accordingly, researchers are developing research methods that allow children to participate as active agents and key informants. This approach provides children with the opportunity to express their feelings and thoughts rather than solely relying on the adult interpretation of their lives. In order to use methods in which children are considered as researchers, children should be empowered.

Core issues of childhood studies

There are three ethical issues in relation to conducting research with children, including power relations, informed consent, and confidentiality. The adult's centeredness in most societies and the unequal power relations between children and adults increase in the research process. This issue leads to the questions of 'do children feel free to refuse to participate in a study or to withdraw during the research?' and 'do they feel free to express their own views and experiences to adult researchers?' Adult researchers are responsible to ensure that children do not suffer harm from participating in research. Participation in the research process may cause children distress and it is the researcher's ethical responsibility to be prepared to deal with any possible negative emotions that may be the result of participating in research (e.g. conflict, guilt, threat to self-esteem, fear of failure, embarrassment).

Informed consent, another ethical issue, is based on three aspects: information giving (gaining knowledge through providing information understandable for children), voluntary participation, and competency (having the capacity to give consent). These issues are emphasized in child-centric research. With respect to information giving, it is difficult to explain the meaning of participation in a research study to children. It is also difficult to convey to children that their participation will likely have no direct benefit to them. Competency is of great concern to researchers because it is unacceptable to only obtain consent from parents, and researchers should continually check whether the child wishes to continue participating.

Confidentiality means that researchers must respect children's privacy and not pressure children into answering questions they do not want to answer. Determining the importance of questions depends on interviewees, not on the interviewer. Researchers have different perspectives on the boundaries of confidentiality in research with children. Some experts say that complete confidentiality cannot be guaranteed and researchers are responsible for protecting the information if they feel a child is at risk.

Research challenges when studying children

- Children cannot perform some physical tasks. Moreover, young children likely cannot operate the electronic measurement devices (such as a people meter) or accomplish a diary or a questionnaire.
- As children's thinking is concrete, it is difficult for them to deal with abstract concepts. They don't always understand what a researcher asks them. They usually have their own definitions of the words and then their own interpretation of research questions. Therefore, it is difficult to construct the research tools that are understandable for all child participants and will lead to clear responses from them.
- Children often have their own unique understanding of environment and time, and thus it is difficult for them to put their experience into a requested frame. For example, their interpretation of 'yesterday' or 'tomorrow' may be different from what the researcher means. They may interpret yesterday as real yesterday (one day ago), a few days ago, or even a few weeks ago. Children also have difficulty in accurately reporting how much time they spent doing something.
- Children's word stock is limited. They have limited vocabularies and it is usually difficult for them to report their thoughts and opinions. Therefore, researchers have problems in determining the reasons for children's wants and behaviors.
- Many children, especially younger ones, do not understand many mathematical concepts well (of course, the same can be true about many adults), such as fractions and percentages. This problem makes it difficult to ask them about proportions and shares.

- Since children's reading skills are limited, there is a problem in constructing questionnaires that they can understand and use correctly. In addition, children with different ages need different instruments, because a questionnaire designed for younger children may be seen as very childish for older children.
- As previously discussed, according to development theories, children learn differently at different ages and stages, and their way of processing information changes as they grow up. This means that what is appropriate for one 7-year-old may be inappropriate for an 11-year-old. This problem increases when research is done across different countries with different cultural and sociological variables. Differences in cognitive development and skill levels should be considered in both researching on and marketing to children of different ages.
- Children's attention spans are limited, and this limits the number of questions the researcher can ask or the number of tasks he or she can give them to do. To deal with this problem, short written and personal interviews are generally best.
- Children are egocentric and do not want to participate in tasks that are irrelevant to them. But most research tasks are more relevant to the researcher than to the children. Therefore, it depends on the researcher's creativity to keep the task and the study interesting for child participants.
- As children's memories are relatively undeveloped, it may be difficult for them to provide answers about things happened in the past.
- Children's sense of responsibility is not strong and thus, they require special motivation to continue their participation in a long-term study. On the other hand, children like to feel that they are responsible. Researchers can use this characteristic to reinforce children's spirit of cooperation.
- Some children are shy and thus it is difficult to elicit answers from them.
- Children have difficulty with volumetric questions. For example, they cannot report how many times they ate a special food in the past month.
- Researchers should be aware of the regulations of different countries about communicating with children and the effects of such regulations on research methods.
- In many studies on children, parents are often interviewed instead of their children and report their children's behavior and preferences inaccurately. But in fact, parents are not always aware of their children's thoughts, preferences, and actions, especially when children are younger (i.e. children under the age of 8 or 9).

Marketing research and children

Compared with adults, children are difficult subjects for market researchers. They are unreliable reporters of their own behavior, children's memory retrieval is poor, and understanding of abstract contents is difficult for them. Still, market research yields good results, so many companies and specialized firms have been successful in researching some aspects of this attractive and growing segment of the market. For example, through interviewing elementary school pupils, Campbell's Soup discovered that although children like soup, they do not like to admit it because they associate the soup with nerds. Therefore, the company reintroduced the 'Campbell kids' in its advertising after a prolonged absence. But this time, the kids were slimmed down and more athletic to reflect an updated, un-nerdy image.

A particularly helpful type of research with children is product testing. These young subjects can provide valuable perspectives on which products will succeed. As an example, one confectionery company uses a Candy Tasters Club, composed of 1,200 children aged 6 to 16, to evaluate its product ideas. Researchers using techniques such as ethnographic research spend time with children or videotape them as they shop. The most successful interviewers are those who try to be child-centric. This means that they act as a friend to the children and through using a variety of projective techniques try to persuade children to express themselves in their own terms.

Children's level of understanding is especially hard to assess. Since children differ in their abilities to process product-related information, advertisers' efforts to persuade them raise many serious ethical issues. As children's cognitive defenses are not sufficiently developed to filter out advertising appeals, changing their brand preferences is easy; something like shooting fish in a barrel. One way for assessing children's message comprehension is to show pictures of children in different scenarios and ask the child subjects to point to the sketch that says what the advertising is trying to get them to do.

Appendix 1

Summary of the United Nations Convention on the Rights of the Child

Article 1: Definition of a child

Children are defined as all people under 18 years of age.

Article 2: Non-discrimination

All rights in the Convention apply to all children without exception, and the State has an obligation to protect children from any and all forms of discrimination including that resulting from their parents or guardian's status.

Article 3: Best interests of the child

All actions concerning the child must be based on his or her best interests.

Article 4: Implementation of rights

The State has an obligation to translate the rights of the Convention into reality.

Article 5: Parental guidance and the child's evolving capacities as he or she grows

The State has a duty to respect the rights and responsibilities of parents and the wider family or others involved in the upbringing of the child in a manner appropriate to the child's evolving capacities.

Article 6: Survival and development

The child has an inherent right to life, and the State has an obligation to ensure to the maximum extent possible the survival and development of the child.

Article 7: Name and nationality

The child has the right to be registered, to have a name from birth and to be granted a nationality. In addition, the child has the right to know and be cared for his or her parents.

Article 8: Preservation of identity

> The State has an obligation to protect and, if necessary, re-establish the basic aspects of the child's identity (name, nationality and family relations).

Article 9: Separation from parents

> The child has the right to live with his or her parents unless it is not deemed to be in his or her best interests; the child has the right to maintain contact with both parents if separated from one or both.

Article 10: Family reunification

> The State has an obligation to foster and enable family reunification where children and parents live in separate countries; the child whose parents live in a different state has the right to maintain personal relations and direct contact with both parents.

Article 11: Illicit transfer and non-return of children from abroad

> The State has an obligation to try to prevent and to remedy the illicit transfer and non-return of children abroad by a parent or third party.

Article 12: The child's opinion

> The child has the right to express an opinion, and to have that opinion taken into account, in any matter or procedure affecting the child, in accordance with his or her age and maturity.

Article 13: Freedom of expression

> The child has the right to obtain and make known information, and to express his or her own views, unless this would violate the rights of others.

Article 14: Freedom of thought, conscience and religion

> The child has the right to freedom of thought, conscience and religion, subject to appropriate parental guidance and national law.

Article 15: Freedom of association

> The child has the right to meet with others and to join or set up associations, unless doing so would violate the rights of others.

Article 16: Protection of privacy

> The child has the right to protection from interference with privacy, family, home and correspondence, and from libel or slander.

Article 17: Access to appropriate information

The State has an obligation to ensure that the child has access to information and material from a diversity of media sources and to take measures to protect children from harmful materials.

Article 18: Parental responsibilities

The State has an obligation to recognize and promote the principle that both parents or legal guardians have common responsibilities for the upbringing and development of the child; the State shall support parents or legal guardians in this task through the provision of appropriate assistance.

Article 19: Protection from abuse and neglect

The State has an obligation to protect children from all forms of abuse and neglect, to provide support to those who have been abused and to investigate instances of abuse.

Article 20: Protection of children without families

The State has an obligation to provide special protection for children without families and to ensure that appropriate alternative family care or institutional placement is made available to them, taking into account the child's cultural background.

Article 21: Adoption

In countries where adoption is recognized and/or allowed, it shall only be carried out in the best interests of the child, with all necessary safeguards for the child and under the authorization of competent authorities.

Article 22: Refugee children

Special protection is to be granted to children who are refugees or seeking refugee status, and the State has an obligation to co-operate with competent organizations providing such protection and assistance.

Article 23: Children with a disability

Children with a mental or physical disability have the right to special care, education and training designed to help them to achieve the greatest possible self-reliance and to lead a full active life in society.

Article 24: Health and health services

The child has the right to the enjoyment of the highest possible standard of health and to have access to healthcare and medical services. In its provision of health services, the State shall place special emphasis on primary and preventative health care and public health education.

Article 25: Periodic review of placement in care settings

The child who has been placed in a care setting by the State for reasons of care, protection or treatment has the right to have all aspects of that placement reviewed and evaluated regularly.

Article 26: Social security

The child has the right to benefit from social security.

Article 27: Growing up free from poverty

The child has the right to an adequate standard of living; parents have the primary responsibility to provide this, and the State has a duty to assist parents, where necessary, in fulfilling this right.

Article 28: Education

The child has the right to education; the State has a duty to make primary education compulsory and free to all; to take measures to develop different forms of secondary education and to make this accessible to all children. School discipline should be administered in a manner consistent with the child's human dignity.

Article 29: Aims of education

Education should be directed at developing the child's personality and talents; preparing the child for active life as an adult; fostering respect for basic human rights; developing respect for the child's own cultural and national values and those of others; and developing respect for the natural environment.

Article 30: Children of minorities or indigenous peoples

Children of minority communities and indigenous peoples have the right to enjoy their own culture, to practice their own religion and to use their own language.

Article 31: Leisure, recreation and cultural activities

The child has the right to rest and to engage in leisure, play and recreational activities and to participate in cultural and artistic activities.

Article 32: Child labour

The State has an obligation to protect children from engaging in work that negatively impacts their health, education or development; to set a minimum age for employment; and to regulate conditions of employment.

Article 33: Drug abuse

The child has a right to protection from illicit use of narcotic and psychotropic drugs and from being involved in their production and distribution.

Article 34: Sexual exploitation

The child has the right to protection from all forms of sexual exploitation and sexual abuse, including prostitution and involvement in pornography.

Article 35: Sale, trafficking and abduction

The State has an obligation to prevent any form of abduction of children or sale of or traffic in children.

Article 36: Other forms of exploitation

The child has the right to protection from all other forms of exploitation prejudicial to their welfare.

Article 37: Torture and deprivation of liberty

The State has an obligation to ensure that no child is subject to torture, cruel, inhuman or degrading treatment or punishment, capital punishment, life imprisonment, and unlawful arrest or deprivation of liberty. A child who is deprived of liberty must be treated with humanity and respect and in a manner that is appropriate to his or her age. Children who are detained should be separated from adults, have the right to contact with family, and access to legal and other assistance.

Article 38: Armed conflicts

The State has an obligation to respect, and to ensure respect for humanitarian law as it applies to children in situations of armed conflict. States must ensure that no child under the age of fifteen can take direct part in hostilities or be recruited into the armed forces. States must take all feasible measures to ensure protection and care of children who are affected by armed conflict.

Article 39: Rehabilitative care

The State has an obligation to take all appropriate measures to promote the physical and psychological recovery and social integration of children who have been victims of any form of neglect, exploitation or abuse, torture or degrading treatment or of armed conflict.

Article 40: Administration of juvenile justice

> Children accused of, or recognized as having committed an offence have the right to respect for their human rights and in particular to benefit from all aspects of the due process of law, including legal or other assistance in preparing and presenting their defence. States have an obligation to promote alternative procedures and measures so as to ensure that recourse to judicial proceedings and institutional placements can be avoided wherever possible and appropriate.

Article 41: Respect for existing standards

> If standards set in the national law of a country which has ratified the Convention, or in other applicable international instruments, are higher than those in the Convention on the Rights of the Child, it is the higher standard that will apply.

Articles 42–45 define how compliance with the Convention is to be monitored and fostered.

Appendix 2
Theories and models

Adaptation level theory (Chapter 3)

Helson developed the adaptation level theory of psychology. This theory states that an individual's basis of judgment on a stimulus is based on their prior experiences as well as their recollections of how they perceived similar stimuli in the past. According to this theory, adaptation levels vary from person to person and in different situations.

Attribution theory (Chapter 4)

Attribution theory explains how individuals interpret events and how their interpretation relates to their thinking and behavior. A psychological theory of attribution was first proposed by Heider, and further advanced by Weiner et al. Attribution theory assumes that people try to attribute causes to other people's behavior. Of course, the attribution happens if the person perceives or observes the behavior, and also he or she believes that the behavior was intentionally performed.

Classical conditioning (Chapter 6)

The classical conditioning theory was proposed by Ivan Pavlov and discusses that behavior is learned by a repetitive association between the response and the stimulus. Classical conditioning occurs when a conditioned stimulus (which is usually a neutral stimulus) is paired with an unconditioned stimulus (which is usually biologically potent). After pairing is repeated, the organism exhibits a conditioned response to the conditioned stimulus even when the unconditioned stimulus is not presented. This theory is based on the assumption that learning is developed through interactions with the environment. Also, it presumes that the environment shapes the behavior, and individuals' internal mental state cannot explain their behavior.

Commodity theory (Chapter 5)

Commodity theory deals with the psychological effects of scarcity and claims that any commodity will be valued to the extent that it is unavailable. Commodity, value, and unavailability are three core concepts of this theory. The concept of commodity refers to any things (such as messages, experiences, or objects) about the usefulness, transferability, and the potential of being possessed of a commodity. Value refers to a commodity's potency for affecting attitudes and behavior. Enhancement of a commodity's value will increase its perceived utility. And finally, unavailability, which is extremely relevant to marketing practice, refers to scarcity and other limits on availability.

Consumer socialization (Chapter 1; Chapter 3)

Consumer socialization is the process by which young people develop consumer-related skills, knowledge, and attitudes.

a)   *Cognitive development theory (Chapter 1; Chapter 2; Chapter 5)*

In the domain of cognition, Jean Piaget's theory has been tremendously influential, suggesting a predictable sequence of stages for cognitive development: sensorimotor, preoperational, concrete operational, and formal operational. Piaget argued that these stages were characterized by qualitatively different modes of thinking through which individuals pass from infancy to adolescence.

b)   *Social development theory (Chapter 1; Chapter 6)*

According to the major theme of Lev Vygotsky's theoretical framework, social interaction plays a fundamental role in the development of cognition. Vygotsky stated that every function in the child's cultural development appears first on the social level (between people) and later on the individual level (inside the child).

c)   *Interpersonal communication theory (Chapter 1)*

Interpersonal communication is an exchange of information between two or more people. There are a variety of interpersonal communication theories, including those that explain how relationships are initiated and developed, theories of how relationships are maintained over time, and theories that explain why and what to do when people behave in ways that are unexpected.

d) *Learning theory (Chapter 1)*

Learning theories are an organized set of principles explaining how people acquire, retain, and recall knowledge. Two major learning theories are cognitive and behavioral learning theories. Cognitive learning theory stresses the importance of internal mental processes, whereas behavioral learning theories assume that learning takes place as the result of responses to external events.

Cue reactivity theory (Chapter 6)

Cue reactivity is a type of learned response that is observed in individuals with an addiction and involves significant physiological and subjective reactions to presentations of drug-related stimuli (i.e. drug cues). This theory is about exposure to a cue or set of cues, such as the smell of a favorite drink, and observation and measurement of a variety of responses.

Cultivation theory (Chapter 4)

Cultivation theory, which was proposed by George Gerbner, deals with the long-term effects of television. This theory assumes that the more time people spend living in the television world, the more likely they are to believe social reality aligns with reality as portrayed on television. Cultivation theory suggests that exposure to media over time subtly cultivates viewers' perceptions of reality. Gerbner and Gross believed that television was a medium of enculturation (i.e. socialization of most people into standardized roles and behaviors).

Dichotomous child theory (Chapter 1)

Dichotomous child theory argues that children can be considered both as passive and vulnerable subjects at the same time and as sort of heroic figures who have the power of making unique and original meanings out of every piece of culture.

Discourse theory (Chapter 5)

Discourse theory states that all the relevant text around a message should be considered to understand it clearly and universally, instead of viewing it as a stand-alone sentence. Discourse theory has received prominence in social sciences. This theory offered a new analytical perspective that focused on the rules and meaning that determine the construction of social, political, and cultural identity.

Ecological systems theory (Chapter 3)

Ecological systems theory offers a framework through which community psychologists examine individuals' relationships within communities and the wider society. This theory states that human development is influenced by the different types of environmental systems and identifies five environmental systems with which an individual interacts, including the microsystem, mesosystem, exosystem, macrosystem, and chronosystem.

Elaboration likelihood model (ELM) (Chapter 3; Chapter 5)

The elaboration likelihood model explains different ways of processing stimuli, why they are used, and their outcomes on attitude change. It assumes that once a person receives a message he or she begins to process it. Under conditions of high involvement, the person takes the central route to persuasion, while under conditions of low involvement, a peripheral route is taken instead.

Food marketing defense model (Chapter 5)

Food marketing defense model is an approach to understanding how food marketing affects young people and the conditions necessary to effectively defend against its negative impact. According to this model, four conditions are needed for individuals to effectively resist food marketing stimuli: awareness of marketing stimuli and comprehension of their persuasive intent; understanding of the effects resulting from exposure to stimuli and of the ways of defending against those effects; ability to effectively resist; and motivation to resist. This model argues that different forms of marketing and different contexts can influence the ability to defend against marketing effects.

Health halo effect (Chapter 5)

Health halos, derived from halo effects theory, explain that a claim about single healthy quality (such as being low in calories or low in fat) gives rise to more positive impression of other, non-claimed qualities. The health halo changes audience's perceptions of the overall healthfulness of certain products through influencing impression formation and judgment of them.

Information processing theory (Chapter 1)

Information processing theory, like the cognitive development theories, is based on the idea that humans process the information they receive rather than merely responding to stimuli. This theory addresses how children's brains likewise mature, leading to advances in their ability to process and respond to the information they received through their senses. The theory emphasizes a continuous pattern of development, in contrast with theories, such as Jean Piaget's cognitive development theory, that considered stages for thought development.

Intergroup relations theory (Chapter 4)

Intergroup relations theory refers to interactions between individuals in different social groups and also between the groups. According to Sherif's definition of intergroup relations, intergroup behavior occurs whenever individuals belonging to one group interact, collectively or individually, with another group or its members in terms of their group identification.

Limited capacity model of attention (Chapter 6)

Limited capacity model of attention, as an explanatory theory, assumes that humans have a limited capacity for cognitive processing of information. The origin of this theory is in psychology. As Kahneman suggested, a limited amount of attention is allocated to tasks by a central processor. Many factors determine how much attentional capacity can be allocated and how much is needed for each task.

Parasocial relationship theory (Chapter 4)

Parasocial interaction (PSI), which was coined by Horton and Wohl, refers to a kind of psychological relationship experienced by an audience in their mediated encounters with performers in the mass media, particularly on television. As this theory describes, audiences consider media figures as friends, despite having limited interactions with them. Horton and Wohl explored the different interactions between mass media users and media figures and determined the existence of a parasocial relationship (PSR), where the user acts as though they are involved in a typical social relationship. According to the use-and-gratifications approaches, the two concepts of PSI and PSR are typically treated interchangeably and emphasize a special type of interpersonal involvement with media figures. However, some other research domains, such as media psychology and semiotics, consider a clear distinction between the two terms. PSI refers to the one-sided process of media figure perception during media exposure (when an audience feels like they are interacting with a media figure), while PSR stands for a cross-situational relationship between the audience and a media figure (when an audience imagines a long-term bond with a media figure), which includes specific cognitive and effective components. In this sense, it is argued that PSI can lead to PSR, and PSR can strengthen PSI.

Pathogen avoidance theory (Chapter 4)

In response to the threat of communicable pathogens, many animal species have evolved immune systems that detect and destroy pathogens when they enter the body. The ability to detect and avoid infection would allow the organism to mate and produce healthy offspring. A sort of behavioral immune system also has evolved, characterized by mechanisms that allow individuals to detect and avoid pathogen-carrying conspecifics. Avoidance of infected conspecifics is observed in many animal species, including humans.

Perceived social consensus model (Chapter 4)

Perceived social consensus refers to the degree to which people in one's social group are in agreement about an issue. Humans, as social creatures, continually perceive others and predict what others think, feel, and, most importantly, what they will do. According to this theory, a population or a society is defined based on common experiences, interests, and values. In order to be effective, social perceptions and predictions must be reasonably accurate. Perceivers' own behavior, values, or their visual perspective uniquely affect their judgments.

Persuasion knowledge model (PKM) (Chapter 6)

Consumers interpret and cope with marketers' sales promotions and advertising. Over time they develop personal knowledge about marketers' attempts, and use this knowledge to identify how, when, and why marketers try to influence them. They also respond to these persuasion attempts using obtained knowledge. Wright informally discussed such persuasion knowledge as a schemer schema. According to persuasion knowledge model, people's persuasion knowledge is developmentally contingent. It continues developing throughout the life span and can be learned through ways including firsthand experiences in social interactions; conversations about effective factors in people's thoughts, feelings, and behaviors; observing marketers; and commentary on advertising and marketing tactics in the news media.

Priming theory (based on associative network model) (Chapter 5)

The priming theory, grounded in cognitive psychology, states that media images stimulate related thoughts in the minds of audience members. This theory has been derived from the associative network model of human memory that assumes knowledge in memory consists of nodes and links and is structured into associative networks. Priming theory refers to the activation of a node in a network, which may serve as a filter, an interpretive frame, or a premise for further information processing or judgment formation.

Russel and Mehrabian's environmental psychology approach (Chapter 3)

Russel and Mehrabian's environmental psychology approach (or PAD [pleasure, arousal, dominance] emotional state model) is a psychological model to describe and measure emotional states. This model uses three dimensions including pleasure, arousal, and dominance to represent all emotions. The initial use of this model was in a theory of environmental psychology, the core idea of which was that physical environments influence people through their emotional impact.

Social cognitive theory (social learning theory) (Chapter 4)

Social cognitive theory (SCT) states that portions of an individual's knowledge acquisition can be directly related to observing others within the context of social interactions, experiences, and outside media influences. According to this theory, which was advanced by Albert Bandura, when people observe certain behavior and its consequences, they remember the sequence of events and use this information to guide subsequent behaviors. Observing a model can prompt the viewer to engage in behavior they already learned. Therefore, people do not learn new behaviors only by trying them and either succeeding or failing, but rather they may learn by observing the actions of others. Depending on whether people are rewarded or punished for their behavior and the outcome of the behavior, the observer may choose to replicate behavior modeled. In 1986 Bandura, based on his studies and findings, decided to rename his social learning theory (SLT) to social cognitive (learning) theory (SCLT).

Social identity theory (Chapter 5)

Social identity argues that people build a part of their self-concept based on the membership in one or more social groups. Tajfel and Turner introduced the concept of a social identity as a way to explain intergroup behavior. Social identity theory is used to predict certain intergroup behaviors based on perceived group status differences; the perceived legitimacy and stability of these differences; and the perceived ability to move from one group to another.

Social power theory (Chapter 1)

This theory illustrates that many complex phenomena about groups can be deduced from a few simple postulates about interpersonal relations. There are three major postulates dealing with the effects of the power structure of the group: a) the power relations among members of the group; b) the communication networks or patterns of interaction in the group; and c) the relations among opinions within the group.

Bibliography

Alvy, L. M., & Calvert, S. L. (2008). Food marketing on popular children's web sites: A content analysis. *Journal of the American Dietetic Association, 108*(4), 710–713.

Ambady, N., Shih, M., Kim, A., & Pittinsky, T. L. (2001). Stereotype susceptibility in children: Effects of identity activation on quantitative performance. *Psychological Science, 12*(5), 385–390.

Andrews, I. C., Netemeyer, R. G., & Burton, S. (2009). The nutrition elite: Do only the highest levels of caloric knowledge, obesity knowledge, and motivation matter in processing nutrition Ad claims and disclosures? *Journal of Public Policy & Marketing, 28*(1), 41–55.

Andronikidis, A. I., & Lambrianidou, M. (2010). Children's understanding of television advertising: A grounded theory approach. *Psychology & Marketing, 27*(4), 299–322.

Bandura, A. (1986). *Social foundations of thought and action: A social cognitive theory*. Englewood Cliffs, NJ: Prentice-Hall.

Bandura, A. (2001). Social cognitive theory of mass communication. *Media Psychology, 3*(3), 265–299.

Bandura, A. (2008). Social cognitive theory of mass communication. In J. Bryant & M. B. Oliver (Eds.), *Media effects: Advances in theory and research* (pp. 94–124). New York: Routledge.

Banister, M. N., & Booth, G. J. (2005). Exploring innovative methodologies for child-centric consumer research. *Qualitative Market Research: An International Journal, 8*(2), 157–175.

Barker, J., & Weller, S. (2003). "Is it fun?" developing children centred research methods. *International Journal of Sociology and Social Policy, 23*(1/2), 33–58.

Bech, A. C., Grunert, K. G., Bredahl, L., Juhl, H. J., & Poulsen, C. S. (2001). Consumers' quality perception. In L. J. Frewer, E. Risvik, & H. N. J. Schifferstein (Eds.), *Food, people and society* (pp. 97–113). New York: Springer.

Berger, C. R. (2008). Interpersonal communication. In W. Donsbach (Ed.), *International encyclopedia of communication* (pp. 3671–3682). New York: Wiley-Blackwell.

Bessenoff, G. B., & Sherman, J. W. (2000). Automatic and controlled components of prejudice toward fat people: Evaluation versus stereotype activation. *Social Cognition, 18*(4), 329–353.

Bond, B. J., & Calvert, S. L. (2014). A model and measure of U.S. parents' perceptions of young children's parasocial relationships. *Journal of Child Media, 8*, 286–304.

Boyland, E. J., Harrold, J. A., Kirkham, T. C., Corker, C., Cuddy, J., Evans, D. . . . Halford, J. C. (2011). Food commercials increase preference for energy-dense foods, particularly in children who watch more television. *Pediatrics, 128*(1), 93–100.

Brock, T. C., & Brannon, L. A. (1992). Liberalization of commodity theory. *Basic and Applied Social Psychology, 13*(1), 135–144.

Bronfenbrenner, U. (2009). *The ecology of human development: Experiments by nature and design.* Cambridge, MA: Harvard University Press.

Brylinsky, J. A., & Moore, J. C. (1994). The identification of body build stereotypes in young children. *Journal of Research in Personality, 28*(2), 170–181.

Buijzen, M. (2009). The effectiveness of parental communication in modifying the relation between food advertising and children's consumption behavior. *British Journal of Developmental Psychology, 27*(1), 105–121.

Busse, P., & Bernabe-Ortiz, A. (2018). Self-regulation of the Peruvian food industry: Health message cues in the context of food and beverage advertisements. *Public Health, 159*, 1–3.

Campbell, M. C., & Mohr, G. S. (2011). Seeing is eating: How and when activation of a negative stereotype increases stereotype-conducive behavior. *Journal of Consumer Research, 38*(3), 431–444.

Campbell, M. S., Manning, K. C., Leonard, B., & Manning, H. M. (2015). Kids, cartoons, and cookies: Stereotype priming effects on children's food consumption. *Journal of Consumer Psychology, 26*(2), 257–264.

Caraher, M., & Landon, J. (2006). The impact of advertising on food choice: The social context of advertising, In R. Shepherd & M. Raats (Eds.), *The psychology of food choice* (pp. 227–245). Wallingford: CABI Publishing.

Carter, B. L., & Tiffany, S. T. (1999). Meta-analysis of cue reactivity in addiction research. *Addiction, 94*(3), 327–340.

Cartwright, K. B. (2001). Cognitive developmental theory and spiritual development. *Journal of Adult Development, 8*(4), 213–220.

Castonguay, J., McKinley, C., & Kunkel, D. (2013). Health-related messages in food advertisements targeting children. *Health Education, 113*(5), 420–432. http://doi.org/10.1108/HE-09-2012-0047.

Chambers, E. (2005). Commentary: Conducting sensory research with children. *Journal of Sensory Studies, 20*(1), 90–92.

Chandon, P. (2013). How package design and packaged-based marketing claims lead to overeating. *Applied Economic Perspectives and Policy, 35*(1), 7–31.

Chaunt, L. (2012). Explicit weight biases are curvilinear: Testing pathogen avoidance, intergroup relations and socialization theories. *Honors Projects Overview, 61*. Retrieved from http://digitalcommons.ric.edu/honors_projects/61.

Chen, K. H., Shen, K. S., & Ma, M. Y. (2012). The functional and usable appeal of Facebook SNS games. *Internet Research, 22*(4), 467–481.

Children's Rights Alliance, Summary of the UN Convention on the Rights of the Child. (2013). Retrieved from www.childrensrights.ie/sites/default/files/information_sheets/files/SummaryUNCRC.pdf.

Chitakunye, P. (2012). Recovering children's voices in consumer research. *Qualitative Market Research: An International Journal, 15*(2), 206–224.

Colman, A. M. (2009). *A dictionary of psychology* (3rd ed.). Oxford: Oxford University Press. Retrieved from www.oxfordreference.com/view/10.1093/oi/authority. 20110803095350211.

Connell, P. M., Brucks, M., & Nielsen, J. H. (2014). How childhood advertising exposure can create biased product evaluations that persist into adulthood. *Journal of Consumer Research, 41*(1), 119–134.

Contento, I. (2008). Nutrition education: Linking research, theory, and practice. *Asia Pacific Journal of Clinical Nutrition, 17*(1), 176–179.

Cook, D. T. (2005). The dichotomous child in and of commercial culture. *Childhood, 12*(2), 155–159.

Cook, D. T. (2008). The missing child in consumption theory. *Journal of Consumer Culture, 8*(2), 219–243.

Cook, D. T. (2009). Knowing the child consumer: Historical and conceptual insights on qualitative children's consumer research. *Young Consumers, 10*(4), 269–282.

Crandall, C. S. (1994). Prejudice against fat people: Ideology and self-Interest. *Journal of Personality and Social Psychology, 66*(5), 882–894.

Deliza, R., & MacFie, H. (2001). Product packaging and branding. In L. J. Frewer, E. Risvik, & H. N. J. Schifferstein (Eds.), *Food, people and society* (pp. 3–7). New York: Springer.

Derbaix, C., & Pecheux, C. (2003). A new scale to assess children's attitude toward TV advertising. *Journal of Advertising Research, 43*(4), 390–399.

Derscheid, L. E., Umoren, J., Kim, S., Henry, B. W., & Zittel, L. L. (2010). Early childhood teachers' and staff members' perceptions of nutrition and physical activity practices for preschoolers. *Journal of Research in Childhood Education, 24*(3), 248–265.

Dias, M., & Agante, L. (2011). Can advergames boost children's healthier eating habits? A comparison between healthy and non-healthy food. *Journal of Consumer Behaviour, 10*(3), 152–160. https://doi.org/10.1002/cb.359.

Dixon, H., Scully, M., Kelly, B., Chapman, K., & Wakefield, M. (2014). Can counter-advertising reduce pre-adolescent children's susceptibility to front-of-package promotions on unhealthy foods?: Experimental research. *Social Science & Medicine, 116*, 211–219.

Dixon, H., Scully, M., Niven, P., Kelly, B., Chapman, K., Donovan, R. . . . Wakefield, M. (2013). Effects of nutrient content claims, sports celebrity endorsements and premium offers on pre-adolescent children's food preferences: Experimental research. *Pediatric Obesity, 9*(2), 47–57.

Dixon, H., Scully, M., & Parkinson, K. (2006). Pester power: Snackfoods displayed at supermarket checkouts in Melbourne, Australia. *Health Promotion Journal of Australia, 17*(2), 124–127.

Dixon, H. G., Scully, M. L., Wakefield, M. A., White, V. M., & Crawford, D. A. (2007). The effects of television advertisements for junk food versus nutritious food on children's food attitudes and preferences. *Social Science & Medicine, 65*(7), 1311–1323.

Dona, G. (2006). Children as research advisors: Contributions to a "methodology of participation" in researching children in difficult circumstances. *International Journal of Migration, Health and Social Care, 2*(2), 22–34.

Drummond, D. C. (2000). What does cue-reactivity have to offer clinical research? *Addiction, 95*(2), 129–144.

Elliott, C. (2012). Packaging health: Examining "better-for-you" foods targeted at children. *Canadian Public Policy, 30*(2), 265–281.

Esmaeilpour, F., Heidarzadeh, K., Mansourian, Y., & Khounsiavash, M. (2017a). Children's experience of overweight cartoon characters in marketing activities: A phenomenological study. *Journal of Business Management, 8*(4), 721–744.

Esmaeilpour, F., Heidarzadeh, K., Mansourian, Y., & Khounsiavash, M. (2017b). *The role of advertising on children's food choice: A mixed method research.* PhD Thesis. Science and Research Branch, Islamic Azad University, Tehran, Iran.

Fiates, G. M. R., Amboni, R. D. M. C., & Teixeira, E. (2008). Television use and food choices of children: Qualitative approach. *Appetite, 50*(1), 12–18.

Folkvord, F., Anschutz, D. J., & Buijzen, M. (2016). The association between BMI development among young children and (un)healthy food choices in response to food advertisements: A longitudinal study. *International Journal of Behavioral Nutrition and Physical Activity, 13*(1), 1–7.

French, J. R. P., Jr. (1956). A formal theory of social power. *Psychological Review, 63*(3), 181–194.

Friestad, M., & Wright, P. (1994). The persuasion knowledge model: How people cope with persuasion attempts. *Journal of Consumer Research, 21*(1), 1–31.

Gerbner, G., Gross, L., Morgan, M., & Signorielli, N. (1986). Living with television: The dynamics of the cultivation process. In J. Bryant & D. Zillman (Eds.), *Perspectives on media effects* (pp. 17–40). Hilldale, NJ: Lawrence Erlbaum Associates.

Goldberg, M. H., van der Linden, S., Leiserowitz, A., & Maibach, E. (2019). Perceived social consensus can reduce ideological biases on climate change. *Environment and Behavior.* https://doi.org/10.1177/0013916519853302.

Gould, S. J., & Gupta, P. B. (2006). Come on down: How consumers view game shows and the products placed in them. *Journal of Advertising, 35*(1), 65–81.

Grabowski, D. (2012). Identity, knowledge and participation: Health theatre for children. *Health Education, 113*(1), 64–79.

Gray, P. O. (2010). *Psychology.* New York: Worth.

Grunert, K. G. (2006). Marketing parameters and their influence on consumer food choice. In R. Shepherd & M. Raats (Eds.), *The psychology of food choice* (pp. 161–177). Wallingford: CABI Publishing.

Hannabuss, S. (2000). Researching into childhood studies. *Library Management, 21*(8), 423–431.

Harker, D., Sharma, B., Harker, M., & Reinhard, K. (2010). Leaving home: Food choice behavior of young German adults. *Journal of Business Research, 63*(2), 111–115.

Harris, J. L., Brownell, K. D., & Bargh, J. A. (2009). The food marketing defense model: Integrating psychological research to protect youth and inform public policy. *Social Issues and Policy Review, 3*(1), 211–271.

Harris, J. L., Schwartz, M. B., & Brownell, K. D. (2010). Marketing foods to children and adolescents: Licensed characters and other promotions on packaged foods in the supermarket. *Public Health Nutrition, 13*(3), 409–417.

Hart, K. H., Bishop, J. A., & Truby, H. (2002). An investigation into school children's knowledge and awareness of food and nutrition. *Journal of Human Nutrition and Dietetics, 15*(2), 129–140.

Hastings, G., McDermott, L., Angus, K., Stead, M., & Thomson, S. (2006). *The extent, nature and effects of food promotion to children: A review of the evidence.* Geneva: World Health Organization.

Hebden, L., King, L., & Kelly, B. (2011). Art of persuasion: An analysis of techniques used to market foods to children. *Journal of Paediatrics and Child Health, 47*(11), 776–782.

Heider, F. (1958). *The psychology of interpersonal relations.* New York: Wiley.

Hernandez, M. D., & Minor, M. S. (2015). False recall of brands in advergames: A cross-country comparison. *Journal of Research in Interactive Marketing, 9*(1), 54–69.

Hoed, R. C. D., & Elliott, C. (2013). Parents' views of supermarket fun foods and the question of responsible marketing. *Young Consumers, 14*(3), 201–215.

Horton, D., & Wohl, R. (1956). Mass communication and para-social interaction: Observation on intimacy at a distance. *Psychiatry, 19*(3), 215–229.

Institute of Medicine. (2006). *Food marketing to children and youth: Threat or opportunity?* Washington, DC: The National Academies Press.

Ironico, S. (2012). The active role of children as consumers. *Young Consumers, 13*(1), 30–44.

John, D. R. (1999). Consumer socialization of children: A retrospective look at twenty-five years of research. *Journal of Consumer Research, 26*(3), 183–213.

Kelder, S. H., Perry, C. L., Klepp, K. I., & Lytle, L. L. (1994). Longitudinal tracking of adolescent smoking, physical activity, and food choice behaviors. *American Journal of Public Health, 84*(7), 1121–1126.

Kelly, B., Chapman, K., King, L., & Hebden, L. (2011). Trends in food advertising to children on free-to-air television in Australia. *Australian and New Zealand Journal of Public Health, 35*(2), 131–134.

Kenkel, D. S. (1991). Health behavior, health knowledge, and schooling. *Journal of Political Economy, 99*(2), 287–305.

Kent, M. P. Dubois, L., Kent, E. A., & Wanless, A. J. (2013). Internet marketing directed at children on food and restaurant websites in two policy environments. *Obesity, 21*(4), 800–807.

Kirk, S. (2007). Methodological and ethical issues in conducting qualitative research with children and young people: A literature review, *International Journal of Nursing Studies, 44*, 1250–1260.

Klimmt, C., Hartmann, T., & Schramm, H. (2006). Parasocial interactions and relationships. In J. Bryant & P. Vorderer (Eds.), *Psychology of entertainment* (pp. 291–313). Mahwah, NJ: Lawrence Erlbaum Associates Publishers.

Kraak, V., & Story, M. (2015). Influence of food companies' brand mascots and entertainment companies' cartoon media characters on children's diet and health: A systematic review and research needs. *Obesity Reviews, 16*(2), 107–126.

Kramer, R., & Schaffer, J. (2014). Intergroup relations. In C. Cooper (Ed.), *Wiley encyclopedia of management* (pp. 1–3). Wiley.

Krueger, J. (1998). On the perception of social consensus. *Advances in Experimental Social Psychology, 30*, 163–240.

Kuhlmeier, V. A., Wynn, K., & Bloom, P. (2003). Attribution of dispositional states by 12-month-olds. *Psychological Science, 14*(5), 402–408.

Lang, A. (2000). The information processing of mediated messages: A framework for communication research. *Journal of Communication, 50*(1), 46–70.

Lapierre, M. A., Brown, A. M., Houtzer, H. V., & Thomas, T. J. (2017). Child-directed and nutrition-focused marketing cues on food packaging: Links to nutritional content. *Public Health Nutrition, 20*(5), 765–773.

Lehu, J. M. (2007). *Branded entertainment: Product placement and brand strategy in the entertainment business*. London: Kogan Page.

Lueg, T. E., & Finney, R. Z. (2007). Interpersonal communication in the consumer socialization process: Scale development and validation. *Journal of Marketing Theory and Practice, 15*(1), 25–39.

Lumbers, M., & Raats, M. (2006). Food choices in later life. In R. Shepherd & M. Raats (Eds.), *The psychology of food choice* (pp. 289–310). Wallingford: CABI Publishing.

Maclean, L., Edwards, N., Garrard, M., Sims-Jones, N., Clinton, K., & Ashley, L. (2009). Obesity, stigma and public health planning. *Health Promotion International, 24*(1), 88–93.

Malloy, T. E., Lewis, B., Kinney, L., & Murphy, P. (2012). Explicit weight stereotypes are curvilinear: Biased judgments of thin and overweight targets. *European Eating Disorders Review, 20*(2), 151–154.

Mansourian, Y. (2015). *Recovering children's voices in qualitative research in the field of the children's literature*. Biennial Congress of Children's Literature. Tehran: Children's Book Council.

Marti-Parreno, J., Aldas-Manzano, J., Curras-Perez, R., & Sanchez-Garcia, I. (2013). Factors contributing brand attitude in advergames: Entertainment and irritation. *Journal of Brand Management, 20*(5), 374–388.

Mazariegos, S., Chacón, V., Cole, A., & Barnoya, J. (2016). Nutritional quality and marketing strategies of fast food children's combo meals in Guatemala. *BMC Obesity, 3*(1), 52.

McGale, S. L., Halford, J. C. G., Harrold, J. A., & Boyland, E. J. (2016). The influence of brand equity characters on children's food preferences and choices. *The Journal of Pediatrics, 177*, 33–38.

McKown, C., & Weinstein, R. S. (2003). The development and consequences of stereotype consciousness in middle childhood. *Child Development, 74*(2), 498–515.

Moon, Y. S. (2013). Examination of health messages in food advertising: A case of South Korea. *Journal of Food Products Marketing, 19*(5), 387–405.

Moschis, G. P. (1985). The role of family communication in consumer socialization of children and adolescents. *Journal of Consumer Research, 11*(4), 898–913.

Moschis, G. P., & Churchill, G. A. (1978). Consumer socialization: A theoretical and empirical analysis. *Journal of Marketing Research, 15*(4), 599–609.

Moskowitz, G. B. (2005). *Social cognition: Understanding self and others*. New York: Guilford Press.

Nabi, R. L., & Sullivan, J. L. (2001). Does television viewing relate to engagement in protective action against crime? A cultivation analysis from a theory of reasoned action perspective. *Communication Research, 28*(6), 802–825.

Naderer, B., Matthes, J., Binder, A., Marquart, F., Mayrhofer, M., Obereder, A., & Spielvogel, I. (2018). Shaping children's healthy eating habits with food placements? Food placements of high and low nutritional value in cartoons, children's BMI, food-related parental mediation strategies, and food choice. *Appetite, 120*, 644–653.

Noble, C., Corney, M., Eves, A., Kipps, M., & Lumbers, M. (2000). Food choice and school meals: Primary schoolchildren's perceptions of the healthiness of foods and the nutritional implications of food choices. *Hospitality Management, 19*(4), 413–432.

Noble, C., Corney, M., Eves, A., Kipps, M., & Lumbers, M. (2003). Food choice and secondary school meals: The nutritional implications of choices based on preference rather than perceived healthiness. *Hospitality Management, 22*(2), 197–215

Norgaard, M. K., Bruns, K., Christensen, P. H., & Mikkelsen, M. R. (2007). Children's influence on and participation in the family decision process during food buying. *Young Consumers, 8*(3), 197–216.

O'Sullivan, T. (2005). Advertising and children: What do the kids think? *Qualitative Market Research: An International Journal, 8*(4), 371–384.

Olsen, A., Kildegaard, H., Gabrielsen, G., Thybo, A. K., & Moller, P. (2012). Measuring children's food preferences: Using pictures in a computerized conjoint analysis. *Journal of Sensory Studies, 27*(4), 264–276.

Paek, H. J., Quilliam, E. T., Kim, S., Weatherspoon, L. J., Rifon, N. J., & Lee, M. (2014). Characteristics of food advergames that reach children and the nutrient quality of the foods they advertise. *Internet Research, 24*(1), 63–81.

Pan, Z., & Kosicki, G. M. (1997). Priming and media impact on the evaluations of the president's performance. *Communication Research, 24*(1), 3–30.

Panic, K., Cauberghe, V., & Pelsmacker, P. D. (2013). Comparing TV ads and advergames targeting children: The impact of persuasion knowledge on behavioral responses. *Journal of Advertising, 42*(2–3), 264–273.

Park, J. H., Schaller, M., & Crandall, C. S. (2007). Pathogen-avoidance mechanisms and the stigmatization of obese people. *Evolution and Human Behavior, 28*(6), 410–414.

Pempek, T. A., & Calvert, S. L. (2009). Tipping the balance: Use of advergames to promote consumption of nutritious foods and beverages by low-income African American children. *Archives of Pediatrics and Adolescent Medicine, 163*(7), 633–637.

Popper, R., & Kroll, J. J. (2005). Issues and viewpoints: Conducting sensory research with children. *Journal of Sensory Studies, 20*(1), 75–87.

Prell, H., Palmblad, E., Lissner, L., & Berg, C. M. (2011). Health discourse in Swedish television food advertising during children's peak viewing times. *Appetite, 56*(3), 607–616.

Puhl, R. M., & Brownell, K. D. (2003). Psychosocial origins of obesity stigma: Toward changing a powerful and pervasive bias. *Obesity Reviews*, *4*(4), 213–227.

Puhl, R. M., & Heuer, Ch. A. (2010). Obesity stigma: Important considerations for public health. *American Journal of Public Health*, *100*(6), 1019–1028.

Puhl, R. M., Schwartz, M. B., & Brownell, K. D. (2005). Impact of perceived consensus on stereotypes about obese people: A new approach for reducing bias. *Health Psychology*, *24*(5), 517–525.

Pulker, C. E., Scott, J. A., & Pollard, C. M. (2018). Ultra-processed family foods in Australia: Nutrition claims, health claims and marketing techniques. *Public Health Nutrition*, *21*(1), 38–48.

Redondo, I. (2012). The effectiveness of casual advergames on adolescents' brand attitudes. *European Journal of Marketing*, *46*(11/12), 1671–1688.

Riddle, K. (2009). *Cultivation theory revisited: The impact of childhood television viewing levels on social reality beliefs and construct accessibility in adulthood.* Conference Papers, International Communication Association, pp. 1–29.

Roeckelein, J. E. (1998). *Dictionary of theories, laws, and concepts in psychology.* Westport, CT: Greenwood Publishing Group.

Roedder, R. L., Didow, N. M., & Calder, B. J. (1978). A review of formal theories of consumer socialization. In K. Hunt & A. Abor (Eds.), *NA: Advances in consumer research* (Vol. 5, pp. 528–534). Ann Arbor, MI: Association for Consumer Research.

Royo-Bordonada, M. Á., Bosqued-Estefanía, M. J., Damián, J., López-Jurado, L., & Moya-Geromini, M. Á. (2016). Nutrition and health claims in products directed at children via television in Spain in 2012. *Gaceta Sanitaria*, *30*(3), 221–226.

Rozin, P. (2006). The integration of biological, social, cultural and psychological influences on food choice. In R. Shepherd & M. Raats (Eds.), *The psychology of food choice* (pp. 19–39). Wallingford: CABI Publishing.

Rubin, A. M., Perse, E. M., & Powell, R. A. (1985). Loneliness, parasocial interaction, and local television news viewing. *Human Communication Research*, *12*(2), 155–180.

Rubin, A. M., & Rubin, R. B. (1985). Interface of personal and mediated communication: A research agenda. *Critical Studies in Mass Communication*, *5*, 36–53.

Russell, C. A., & Buhrau, D. (2015). The role of television viewing and direct experience in predicting adolescents' beliefs about the health risks of fast-food consumption. *Appetite*, *92*, 200–206.

Sabino, D. (2002). Changing families, changing kids. *Young Consumers*, *4*(1), 9–12.

Schifferstein, H. N. J., Frewer, L. J., & Risvik, E. (2001). Introduction. In L. J. Frewer, E. Risvik & H. N. J. Schifferstein (Eds.), *Food, people and society* (pp. 3–7). New York: Springer.

Schor, J. (2014). *Born to buy: The commercialized child and the new consumer culture.* New York: Scribner.

Shrum, L. J. (1995). Assessing the social influence of television: A social cognitive perspective on cultivation effects. *Communication Research*, *22*(4), 402–429.

Sikorski, C., Luppa, M., Kaiser, M., Glaesmer, H., Schomerus, G., König, H. H., & Riedel-Heller, S. G. (2011). The stigma of obesity in the general public and its implications for public health: A systematic review. *BMC Public Health, 11*(661). Retrieved from www.biomedcentral.com/1471-2458/11/661.

Solomon, D., & Peters, J. (2006). Resolving issues in children's research. *Young Consumers, 7*(1), 68–73.

Solomon, M. R. (2009). *Consumer behavior: Buying, having, and being* (8th ed.). Englewood Cliffs, NJ: Prentice Hall.

Solomon, M. R. (2018). *Consumer behavior: Buying, having, and being* (12th ed.). London: Pearson Education.

Sparrman, A. (2009). Ambiguities and paradoxes in children's talk about marketing breakfast cereals with toys. *Young Consumers, 10*(4), 297–313.

Sramova, B., & Pavelka, J. (2017). The perception of media messages by preschool children. *Young Consumers, 18*(2), 121–140.

Straubhaar, J., LaRose, R., & Davenport, L. (2013). *Media now: Understanding media, culture, and technology* (8th ed.). Boston, MA: Cengage Learning.

Stutts, M. A., Zank, G. M., Smith, K. H., & Williams, S. A. (2011). Nutrition information and children's fast food menu choices. *The Journal of Consumer Affairs, 45*(1), 52–86.

Sullivan, S. A., & Birch, L. L. (1990). Pass the sugar, pass the salt: Experience dictates preference. *Developmental Psychology, 26*(4), 546–551.

Tajfel, H., & Turner, J. C. (1986). The social identity theory of intergroup behaviour. In S. Worchel & W. G. Austin (Eds.), *Psychology of Intergroup Relations* (pp. 7–24). Chicago, IL: Nelson-Hall.

Tarabashkina, L., Quester, P. G., & Crouch, R. (2017). Children and energy-dense foods: Parents, peers, acceptability or advertising?. *European Journal of Marketing, 51*(9/10), 1669–1694.

Tomlinson, A. (2010). *A dictionary of sports studies*. Oxford: Oxford University Press.

Torfing, J. (2005). Discourse theory: Achievements, arguments, and challenges. In D. Howarth & J. Torfing (Eds.) *Discourse theory in European politics* (pp. 1–32). London: Palgrave Macmillan.

Trijp, H. C. M., & Meulenberg, M. T. G. (1996). Marketing and consumer behaviour with respect to foods. In H. L. Meiselman & H. J. H. MacFie (Eds.), *Food choice, acceptance and consumption* (pp. 264–292). London: Chapman and Hall.

Turner, J., & Oakes, P (1986). The significance of the social identity concept for social psychology with reference to individualism, interactionism and social influence. *British Journal of Social Psychology, 25*(3), 237–252.

United Nations (1989). *Convention on the rights of the child*. Retrieved from www.ohchr.org/en/professionalinterest/pages/crc.aspx.

Valkenburg, P. M., & Cantor, J. (2001). The development of a child into a consumer. *Journal of Applied Developmental Psychology, 22*(1), 61–72.

Vashisht, D., & Sreejesh, S. (2015). Effects of brand placement strength, prior game playing experience and game involvement on brand recall in advergames. *Journal of Indian Business Research, 17*(3), 292–312.

Vygotsky, L. S. (1978). *Mind in society*. Cambridge, MA: Harvard University Press.

Waiguny, M. J. K., Nelson, M. R., & Terlutter, R. (2012). Entertainment matters! The relationship between challenge and persuasiveness of an advergame for children. *Journal of Marketing Communications, 18*(1), 69–89.

Ward, S. (1974). Consumer socialization. *Journal of Consumer Research, 1*(2), 1–14.

Weiner, B. (1974). *Achievement motivation and attribution theory*. Morristown, NJ: General Learning Press.

Weiner, B. (1986). *An attributional theory of motivation and emotion*. New York: Springer-Verlag.

Weller, R. F., Marley, C. L., & Moorby, J. M. (2007). Effects of organic and conventional feeding regimes and husbandry methods on the quality of milk and dairy products. In J. Cooper, U. Niggli, & C. Leifert (Eds.), *Handbook of organic food safety and quality* (pp. 97–116). London: Woodhead Publishing Ltd.

Whalen, R., Harrold, J., Child, S., Halford, J., & Boyland, E. (2018). The health halo trend in UK television food advertising viewed by children: The rise of implicit and explicit health messaging in the promotion of unhealthy foods. *International Journal of Environmental Research and Public Health, 15*(3), 560.

Wilks, N. A. (2009). *Marketing food to children and adolescents: A review of industry expenditures, activities, and self-regulation*. New York: Nova Science Publishers.

Williams, J., Wake, M., Hesketh, K., Maher, E., & Waters, E. (2005). Health-related quality of life of overweight and obese children. *Journal of the American Medical Association, 293*(1), 70–76.

Williams, L. A., & Burns, A. C. (2000). Exploring the dimensionality of children's direct influence attempts. *Advances in Consumer Research, 27*(1), 64–71.

Williams, P. (2005). Consumer understanding and use of health claims for foods. *Nutrition Science and Policy, 63*(7), 256–264.

Wise, K., Bolls, P. D., Kim, H., Venkataramn, A., & Meyer, R. (2008). Enjoyment of advergames and brand attitudes: The impact of thematic relevance. *Journal of Interactive Advertising, 9*(1), 27–36.

Index

Note: Page numbers in *italic type* indicate figures or illustrations; those in **bold** indicate tables.

Printed in the United States
by Baker & Taylor Publisher Services